Bethany Hamilton's story of a shark attack while surfing in Hawaii is nothing short of inspiring. The family "story behind the story" may be even more compelling. I loved reading about the Hamilton's life before, during and after the shark attack and how they turned a tragedy into a triumph.

Jim Burns, PhD
President, HomeWord
Author of *10 Building Blocks for a Solid Family* and *Faith Conversations for Families*

If you are a mother, you *must* read this book. Cheri reminds us that our children really belong to God. It is He who lets them breathe, He who knows how many hairs are on their heads, and He who is with them always . . . even when they are in the mouth of a shark.

Shelene Bryan
Founder of Skip1.org , Producer of *Like Dandelion Dust*

Raising a Soul Surfer is an amazing story of how God shows us, even through adversity, that there is triumph. There is hope to those who seek Him, and His love endures forever! As parents, we all have hopes and dreams for our children, yet as big as our plans are for them, they are so much smaller than God's! Through what could have been a devastating tragedy, the Hamilton family has shown that all things do work together for good to those that love Him (see Romans 8:28).

Barbara Cameron
Author of *A Full House of Growing Pains*

This engaging autobiography chronicles the story of an unusual family of surfers that resulted in the phenomenon of Bethany Hamilton. Anyone interested in Bethany's story, surfing or Hawaii in general will enjoy this lighthearted but truthful account of the lives of Tom and Cheri Hamilton, a couple of serious surfers who fell in love in Kauai, lived in a van, and raised their kids surfing from the time they were tadpoles. The drive and dedication the Hamiltons bring to their faith and surfing are showcased in this inspiring story in readable prose that will bring both chuckles and tears.

Toby Neal, LCSW
Therapist, Parent and Author

Spending time with Cheri Hamilton and the whole Hamilton clan during script development, pre-production, filming and beyond gave me a unique perspective on the family. Seeing their love for God and the love of God pouring out of them kept us focused on the true reason for producing the film *Soul Surfer*. Having the opportunity to have Cheri capture even more of the story in *Raising a Soul Surfer* helps fill in all the blanks that are left unfilled by a two-hour movie.

Rich Peluso
Vice President, AFFIRM Films/Sony Pictures Entertainment

I have been truly honored to know Bethany Hamilton, riding with her and sharing platforms where we witness people's hearts being deeply moved by her inspirational story and her faith in God. As a child going and growing through difficulties of having no limbs since birth, I understand the importance of a mother's role in one's life through storms that seem too big at times. Cheri Hamilton's testimony will touch and challenge anyone's perspective of life. Furthermore, her love for Bethany, her family and, above all, God will ignite a flame of faith and encouragement to all who read it.

Nick Vujicic
Founder, Life Without Limbs

RAISING A SOUL SURFER

ONE FAMILY'S EPIC TALE

RAISING A

soul surfer

CHERI HAMILTON
& Rick Bundschuh

Regal

From Gospel Light
Ventura, California, U.S.A.

Published by Regal
From Gospel Light
Ventura, California, U.S.A.
www.regalbooks.com
Printed in the U.S.A.

Cover photograph of Bethany by Noah Hamilton of Noah Hamilton Photography
(www.noahhamiltonphoto.com). Cover photograph of the Hamilton family by Mike
Coots of Mike Coots Photography (www.mikecoots.com).

All photographs © the Hamilton family archive and Noah Hamilton Photography,
except photo #9 (Hamilton family photo) © Steve Gnazzo of Kilohana Photography and
photo #20 (Timmy bodyboarding) © Shea Sevilla. Used with permssion.

Library of Congress Cataloging-in-Publication Data
Hamilton, Cheri.
Raising a soul surfer : one family's epic tale / Cheri Hamilton with Rick Bundschuh.
p. cm.
ISBN 978-0-8307-5969-9 (hard cover)
1. Hamilton, Bethany—Family.
2. Surfing—Wounds and injuries—Hawaii—Kauai—Biography.
3. Shark attacks—Hawaii—Kauai—Biography.
4. Amputees—Rehabilitation—Biography.
5. Christian biography—United States. I. Bundschuh, Rick, 1951- II. Title.
III. Title: One family's epic tale.
GV838.H36H37 2011
797.32092—dc22
[B]
2011007024

Rights for publishing this book outside the U.S.A. or in non-English languages are
administered by Gospel Light Worldwide, an international not-for-profit ministry.
For additional information, please visit www.glww.org, email info@glww.org, or write to
Gospel Light Worldwide, 1957 Eastman Avenue, Ventura, CA 93003, U.S.A.

To order copies of this book and other Regal products in bulk quantities,
please contact us at 1-800-446-7735.

contents

Foreword

"Don't look down," Bethany called out to me as we were surfing a reef break named "Freddy's" on the North Shore of Oahu. I kept eyeing the shadows and coral heads beneath the surface of the crystal-blue water, secretly convinced I had seen a shark. Bethany, in her chill, all-knowing manner, knew exactly what was in my mind and encouraged me to set aside my fears.

If you are that worried about sharks, don't surf. Fear can ruin a good time, and anticipating the unknown is futile. Ever since a shark attacked Bethany, she focuses on what she can control instead of what she can't see. In fact, "Don't Look Down" seems to be an unspoken motto for the entire Hamilton family. This expression is not a suggestion that they ignore their fears; rather, it is a statement of courage that motivates them to embrace life's challenges. Instead of worrying about what *might* happen, the Hamiltons trust in the Lord and don't blink an eye to transitory disturbances. They continue to look up toward the Lord, hoping and praying for good instead of mulling over their fears.

This unique family lives a beautifully rough island life, "following their bliss" and not fretting over what is around the next turn. Rather than analyzing and contemplating their next move, they taste life and experience it. This attitude represents an island mentality of living life to the fullest and simply enjoying the gifts God provides: the ocean, family and friends.

The Hamiltons and the island on which they live (Kauai) are all about community. But it's a kind of community that cannot be replicated. The ocean spiritually bonds people on Kauai. The desire and love for the ocean is in the heart of every Hamilton and seems to carry them from day to day, giving physically satisfying meaning to their lives.

During the past year, I've had time to get to know each member, and at this point they feel like extended family. I have found that although each of the Hamiltons has a love for the ocean, the similarities stop there. Tom (Dad) reminds me of a soft-spoken giant. He anchors the family, but he has the most kindhearted voice you'll ever hear. When I was staying at the Hamilton house during this past winter break, I went with Tom on their little boat to watch Bethany surf some big waves. I've never seen Tom grin so wide. He literally became so entranced by the enormous sets rolling in and the barrel-rides being caught that the boat almost capsized.

If one person could be the entire "coconut wireless," it would be Cheri Hamilton. Cheri never stops praying. When we were shooting a particularly dangerous shark-attack sequence one day, the crew and cast experienced sharp reefs, unruly waves, rising tides and a difficult setup. But in the midst of crewmembers running around and pandemonium setting in, Cheri gathered a few people on the set and prayed for safety. When tensions were high on set and a million different activities consumed every second, it was nice to know that someone was praying for God to watch over every move.

Noah, the oldest son, is the classic firstborn. He is always two steps ahead of the family, and usually most of the people around him as well. He dealt with just about every issue that came up on set, and because of his proactive nature, he, along with his wife, Becky, helped to make the film more accurate. *Soul Surfer* had a relatively low budget, and the production company didn't have finances for an on-set still photographer. So Noah, a professional photographer himself, offered his services. Becky, who has a multitude of high-level skills, also documented the action with their video camera. Now we have images of the cast and crew hard at work—a recorded behind-the-scenes documentary. Noah continually thinks of how to solve problems himself instead of relying on others to do the job. By now he feels like an older brother, and with all of his ingenuity and kindness, he will make a wonderful father to his soon-to-be-born baby!

Tim Hamilton, the middle child, has the disposition of a turtle. In Hawaii, that is a compliment! He is a natural waterman and is most content there. The first time I met Timmy was in the ocean. I had my first surf lesson with Bethany's surf coach, Russell Lewis, and Tim was out in the water playing "lifeguard" for me. Of course, Tim didn't have to look out for me—the film producers could have hired someone—but he took some prime bodyboard time to help me out. Tim lends a quiet hand whenever the need arises . . . never needing to be asked. Even though he says the least in the family, you have to keep your ears wide open around him. Tim is the person most worth listening to for his witty under-the-breath humor, which always makes me chuckle.

And now, Bethany . . . It is difficult to find words to explain my love and admiration for my friend and personal hero. She totally charges![1] I still do not understand how she pops up on such a little short board with one arm. I take for granted her tenacity and trust in God, because that's just the way she is. You cannot begin to compare her to anyone else on this planet. Bethany's godly behavior and playful determination have continually had a positive influence on my life and the lives of those around her.

I remember one particularly windy day when I wanted to surf. Bethany was available, so she took me out surfing. As soon as we arrived at the beach, I regretted my decision. The waves looked more intimidating than anything I had previously surfed before, not to mention it was close to sunset (of course, sharks eat at all hours of the day, so time should be irrelevant for me). Bethany eventually convinced me that I had "definitely ridden bigger waves," so I paddled out.

I was terrified. To me the waves seemed immense and life threatening, while to Bethany they probably seemed tame and barely large enough to have fun on. At one point, I endured a particularly gnarly wipeout (for me at least), but I'll forever be proud of the small scar the fin of my board carved on my leg. After my wipeout, I caught the longest and most enjoyable right of my surf career to date.[2]

After the ride was over, I couldn't wipe the smile off my face. And I have Bethany to thank—she pushed me and taught me not to "look down." Because she believed in me, I achieved a wave I never thought possible. Her presence ignites a vigor for life that is unique to anyone I have ever met.

Bethany, Timmy, Noah, Cheri and Tom, I want to thank you for welcoming me into your lives. You have shared with me your love for the ocean, so I want to share with you one of my favorite quotes that captures our beloved sea: "Unchangeable save to thy wild waves' play . . . roll on, thou deep and dark blue Ocean—roll."[3]

AnnaSophia Robb

Notes

1. "Charges": having no fear and going for big waves.
2. "Right": A wave breaking toward the right from the vantage point of the surfer riding the wave. From the beach it would be a wave breaking toward the left.
3. Lord Byron, "Apostrophe to the Ocean," *Childe Harold's Pilgrimage.*

Introduction

Greater love has no one than this,
that he lay down his life for his friends.

JOHN 15:13

Tom, my husband, and my daughter, Bethany, had gone to Puerto Rico for a surf competition. Sitting at the computer, I did a search for weather conditions. That region tends to get big storms. I became concerned when I found hurricane Shary brewing, which is my name but with a different spelling. The weather report also said that another hurricane, called Tomas, my husband's name, followed back to back and had stormed over Hamilton, an island town in Bermuda.

I was amazed at the irony of the names, because it described in weather terms what life has been like for our family. At this time, November 2010, our nephew had just died on the East coast, and here on Kauai, everyone was in shock over the death of four-time world champion surfer Andy Irons, who had lived close by.

All of these unusual signs also acted as a confirmation to put down on paper my reflections of the storm-surging changes that have come upon my life and that of my family, as well as the Island of Kauai.

My mother said that I didn't walk at seven months, I ran! Activity and energy have been a part of me from the start. I should have been a pro athlete, but at the time there were few options for women.

When I went surfing for the first time, my life was never the same. I soon committed my whole life and existence to catching the next wave. For the next 15 years, I lived to surf. I focused my everyday life on finding waves and only working jobs that allowed me to have time to surf.

When I met Jesus, I personally experienced His divine providence in a way that I could not walk away from, which guaranteed that I would never deny His existence. After I had invited Jesus into my heart, I knew that I had found the truth and, at last, that my deepest desire for love was fulfilled and complete in Him. His love filled a void in my heart that I had longed for all of my life.

At the beginning, I was a young surfer girl, living my dreams, who encountered God in an unlikely place through unlikely disciples. I was a surf gypsy, with a surf gypsy husband, enjoying life in a tropical paradise. But I became a mother who had to wrestle with fear and uncertainty when the news came that her daughter had been attacked by a shark. I never expected our children to be life-changers. We had raised our daughter to surf, not to be in the media spotlight. Yet she embraced this challenge to honor God and be His witness to the world.

Our story is about a violently shattered dream that was replaced with a bigger one. But most of all, our life story has been, and continues to be, about trusting God in spite of circumstances, pressures and unexpected events.

I've always wanted to be involved in some kind of Christian ministry, but every door closed for me; so I focused on raising my children for Him—teaching them His Word, His ways and His unconditional love. Unbelievably, it turned out to be the very ministry God was calling me to all along.

My story tells about a journey to find hope, truth and purpose. It encompasses the perspective of my husband, a sensitive yet strong father who struggled to make sense of a tragedy, and who had to learn to trust God all over again. It reveals my struggles to find love, hope and acceptance. It includes the perspective of my sons, Bethany's brothers, whose lives have been irrevocably changed by the sudden and unforeseen reverberations stemming from the choice our family made to allow Bethany's story to be told.

Most of all, this story is a glimpse into God's perspective as it has been revealed to us. Only in retrospect have we been able to see how far back His amazing providence has reached into our lives. His hand has always been active, and not just since the events of that fateful Halloween morning in 2003. From the beginning, God prepared our lives in so many ways for "such a time as this," just as He did for Queen Esther (Esther 4:14, *NIV*).

My hope is that by reading our story you will be encouraged to pursue God regardless of the cost. He doesn't take away or allow you to go through pain to hurt you, but to heal and transform and draw you to Himself. God's plan is not to leave us as He found us, but to fill our lives with His purpose and His hope for an amazing future filled with His love!

I cannot get enough of God's Word. The more I learn, the more I want to learn. His Word is so deep, fascinating and layered with insight and guidance that it is new to me every morning. God's Word is a book that can be read for a lifetime without ever plumbing its depths. It is filled with the story of His love for each and every person that He has ever created. His Word tells us about hope and a future plan He has for everyone (see Jeremiah 29:11).

One of my favorite Scriptures, in which I put my hope, is, "No eye has seen, no ear has heard, and no mind has imagined what God has prepared for those who love him" (1 Cor. 2:9, *NLT*). I like to encourage others with the words of Psalm 37:4: "Take delight in the LORD, and he will give you your heart's desires" (*NLT*).

When I turned to Christ, I found a love in Him so pure, so perfect and so real that I wanted with all of my heart for everyone to know His amazing love too. My true purpose in life is that I want to share Jesus with the whole world.

I write these words 30 years after I accepted His grace into my life. Through all of the pain and the joy, I still revel in the wonder of His love. I invite you to see the extraordinary things God has done in our *Ohana* and become a part of it as you say yes to God and His perfect love for you!

Cheri Hamilton
Kauai, Hawaii

Hollywood Comes to Paradise

*Now to him who is able to do immeasurably
more than all we ask or imagine.*

EPHESIANS 3:20, *NIV*

"Surreal!" Tom said.

That is the word my husband used a lot to describe the swirl of events that have swept up our family during the last seven years. This was the word he used on a recent spring morning to describe what took place on the pristine, exclusive grounds of Oahu's Turtle Bay Resort.

Turtle Bay is much like the five-star resort on Kauai that Tom has worked at as a waiter for so many years; but now he was waiting in a golf cart for his partner. As usual, he had one eye on the crystal-blue waves peeling along the point.

He smiled and made room for his partner. He had never met this man until today, but he couldn't shake the feeling that he already knew him.

As the bagmen loaded up the cart, they meekly approached Tom's golfing partner. "Excuse me, sir," one of them said, gesturing toward two golfers standing off to the side, resplendent in their Ping shirts, Callaway saddle shoes and Adidas gloves.

"Those gentlemen over there are wondering if they could join you two this morning."

Tom's partner was gracious, but shook his head. "Tell those guys, no offense, but I just want to spend some time with my friend Tom."

Then, actor Dennis Quaid, who had been hired to play the role of Tom in the movie *Soul Surfer* that was about to start filming, slid into the driver's seat of the golf cart and spun the ignition switch. Off they went.

Tom tried to remember the movies he'd seen this iconic American actor in over the years: *The Rookie, Dragonheart, Far From Heaven, The Big Easy, Vantage Point, Flight of the Phoenix, Yours, Mine and Ours* . . .

My husband thought he wouldn't be able to get over the fact that Dennis Quaid wanted to spend the morning hanging out with him, but as the day progressed, a connection grew between them that went beyond a Hollywood actor researching a role. It shifted toward a friendship.

Dennis started out with a little notepad, which Tom figured he was going to use to record notes as he studied him. But after a few minutes, he put it down and never touched it again. As they made the rounds on the beautiful, tropical golf course, Dennis peppered Tom with questions about our family and about raising our kids in Hawaii. He talked freely about his career and about those whose film work he admired.

He also discussed his own family. As someone who had faced family tragedy himself, Dennis talked about the well-reported time when hospital staff mistakenly gave his 10-day-old twins a dosage of heparin 1,000 times the common amount for infants, almost killing them.

Tom listened quietly as the persona of an actor and Hollywood personality melted away and Dennis simply became a loving father who had nearly lost his precious children.

Dennis explained, between the sand traps and putting greens, how he had ended up playing the role of my husband for the movie. "I was playing with my kids on the living room floor one morning when your daughter, Bethany, came on a television show. I remembered that a shark had attacked her. I turned up the volume. When I heard what she had to say, I realized what an amazing young girl she was. Her story touched and inspired me more deeply than you can know. When the show's host said there was a movie in the works about Bethany, I thought, *Now that's something I'd like to be a part of.*

Tom said that Dennis got quiet, even misty-eyed, as he recounted it. Tom could sense the power of the moment and remained silent.

When Dennis spoke again, he turned to Tom and grinned that famous, bright grin and said, "Wouldn't you know it, a few weeks later my agent called and told me that the producers were wondering if I would like to be part of a movie about an impressive girl named Bethany Hamilton from the Hawaiian island of Kauai. I jumped at the chance!"

Tom said then, and again when he got home, "It was a God thing."

In our wildest dreams, neither Tom nor I could have imagined the events that have unfolded in our lives, nor could we have imagined the path our journey would take as a family. I don't mean just the well-known shark attack on an early Halloween morning in 2003. I mean all of the many paths and events that brought us through that near-tragic point and to the present where Tom was playing golf with a talented actor who would be using his talents to tell our story.

I knew beyond a shadow of a doubt that if I had been in charge of writing the script of our lives, I would have written it much differently than God did. But God's script is certainly more incredible! I would describe it as like standing behind a tapestry of God's creation. From my vantage point, I can't see the pattern or the purpose. Life is often stormy, conflicting and seemingly senseless, like the aftermath of a hurricane. Then, every once in a while, God lets me see the front side of the tapestry.

I know that even my husband's playing golf with Dennis Quaid, and the way Dennis seemed to have been summoned to play the part of Tom, has been God-orchestrated. For example, Tom had no idea as he shared his faith in Christ that the actor had been raised in a Christian home and Dennis had made strong statements about his own Christian faith.[1]

It was *all* a God thing; divine providence!

We had waited a long time, seven years, for the day of filming *Soul Surfer* to arrive. But, finally, everything was in place, and in February 2010, our family moved to a house in front of a popular North Shore surf spot called V-land, on Oahu, for the production of the movie.

We were in the epicenter of the surfing world, in the part of Hawaii known as the Seven Mile Miracle, named for the string of world-famous surf breaks found there, such as Pipeline, Sunset Beach and Waimea Bay. The North Shore is where the majority of big wave contests are held and where pros go to train. Others migrate to these prime waves just for the pure passion and love of the sport of surfing. Many others with iron-willed grit challenge the bigger waves the size of multi-story houses grinding into shallow, razor-sharp reefs. If you've ever seen footage of a big-wave surf competition, 9 times out of 10, you're looking at the Seven Mile Miracle.

Moving into our new home for the next couple of months included shipping Hana, our dog, over from our home on Kauai, so that the family would be complete. We could cook our own food and eat together as a family versus staying in a hotel room. We could also have family meetings about the production work in progress. We could even spin up the road on Sunday to attend church with our friends at North Shore Fellowship after an early morning surf session.

In case you were wondering what kind of Hollywood perks we got . . . it didn't include maid service. That was my *kuleana*, or responsibility, although everyone pitched in! Sometimes while Tom was out playing golf with the likes of Dennis Quaid, I played "mother hen" at home.

The making of *Soul Surfer* was not my first time on a set, but I'll admit I'd hardly paid any attention to the many movies in production on Kauai, because the surf always took precedence on my radar.

Our home island, Kauai, and in particular, the North Shore where we live, has been featured in dozens of major movies—such as *South Pacific, Jurassic Park, Raiders of the Lost Ark, Outbreak*—and most recently, *Pirates of the Caribbean: On Stranger Tides*. When the scenic taro fields of Hanalei in *Uncommon Valor* were turned into rice paddies for the Viet Nam effect, we could just pretend Kauai was under attack on our way to go surfing!

I remember the time, just before hurricane Iniki hit, when I was driving past some giant green gates in the middle of a cane field that read "Jurassic Park" on the gates, and wondering what in the world a "Jurassic Park" was. I'd never even heard of it. But now, the production of *Soul Surfer* had at last become a reality. We, as a family, were all in the thick of it. Tom, Bethany and I watched and learned the involved process of making a movie. Through this very rare opportunity of seeing a production team working together to create the story about our family, we came to the set each day. Noah and Becky were hired as co-producers to help fine-tune many important details, some small and others very big. They were involved intimately in and made a difference in casting, locations and music.

In a movie theater, the action moves along quickly; but in order to create those fast-paced, fluid scenes, there is a massive amount of work and time to get it just right. Making a movie is meticulously detailed work. The daily expenses of making a movie required long workdays to take advantage of the good weather. Every tiny nuance is elaborated on, which sometimes takes weeks even before the actual filming begins! We filmed for two months on Oahu, a few days on Kauai, and a week in Tahiti. Every detail in the script, every rewrite—and every rewrite of a rewrite—every contract detail took up most of everyone's time and energy. Once the official filming began, it was exciting to watch; and on occasion, we were able to contribute a tip here and there.

Sean McNamara, the director, who is so talented and has such a congenial personality, did not need too many tips. His creative talent made the whole production a positive, family-friendly movie.

It was fascinating to watch the scenes being shot, but it was also sometimes difficult from a mom's and dad's perspective. One time, we came to the set late in the morning when they were filming a scene at the Hamilton house, just when the family was giving thanks at the meal. Ross, who played our son Noah, didn't know what to do when they all took hands to give thanks. AnnaSophia, who played Bethany, saw his discomfort and placed his hand on her shoulder. I had just looked into the monitor to watch, and I broke! I started crying because the scene was so realistic.

Tim, Bethany's brother, was hired to be a part of the camera crew. He had an asset envied by all—huge calves! When you are filming a surf movie, it means beaches with soft sand. No one wants to carry heavy equipment for long distances across soft sand. But wait! Look at those calves! They can go anywhere! Do anything we ask! Go, Timmy, go! We need you!

God had pre-prepared Tim for years to do a fine job for his sister's movie. He had already made two body boarding DVDs and short films full of humor, creativity, and storytelling. Tim's prowess in the water is legendary. He is as strong as an ox in and out of the water. He already had a reputation for super endurance, boldness and fearlessness in all his endeavors. He went on to be an assistant on the *Hawaii 5-0* TV drama. He has a huge amount of talent and I am thankful as a mother that God has chosen to use him.

We were very happy with the cast of exceptional actors. We as a family were concerned because they needed to be convincing as real surfers in the water. But no need to worry!

Dennis Quaid was caught up by the surfing passion. That meant that not only did Dennis look good in the water on a surfboard, but he also didn't need to act! At one point, Dennis kidded that my husband had ruined him as a golfer by introducing him to surfing. His heart was fully immersed and caught up by riding waves. For the rest of his time on Oahu, he surfed as much as possible even until the day he had to ride his last wave at Makaha and head for the airport while still wet!

Helen Hunt, whose job it was to play my "surf mom" role, was already an avid surfer and brought her own favorite surfboard to use in the movie. On our few days off, we would all go surf longboards. She really has great grace and poise as she drops down the face of a wave. The hottest surfer was Helen's surf coach, "Turtle," who outshined us all! He costarred in the retro classic surf movie *North Shore*. One of my favorite lines in the movie is when she said no to night surfing but then changed her mind. I often did the same thing.

The most significant role in the movie went to AnnaSophia Robb, who plays my daughter, Bethany. Not only did Anna-Sophia have to look like a natural surfer, but she also had to surf with one arm behind her back!

When Bethany and I saw *The Bridge to Terabithia* starring AnnaSophia, we both agreed that she was the perfect actress to play the part. One area we felt was important to accurately portray was how Bethany adapted so amazingly after what should have been a debilitating loss. The shark took Bethany's left arm all the way up to the shoulder. Most of us don't realize just how difficult it is to do the simple little chores of life without a limb. Buttoning a shirt, tying shoes, making lunch—all the everyday things that most people do without thinking about it.

AnnaSophia had highly skilled teachers for the surfing scenes. Her Oahu coach was big wave surfer Noah Johnson. Noah was the surfing stunt double riding the amazing barrel at Pipeline in the movie *Blue Crush*. He is a well-known big wave surfer on the North Shore of Oahu and won the Quicksilver Eddie Aikau big wave competition at Waimea Bay back in January 1, 1999.[2] On Kauai, AnnaSophia worked with Bethany's own world-famous surf coach Russell Lewis, who sets up his lessons out of Hanalei Surf Company. (He is a former Australian Junior Champion.)

AnnaSophia was a quick study for surfing, partly because she'd been involved with dance, gymnastics and swimming in school. She is a natural athlete like her father and has the gracious charm of her mother. We gave her an A+ as a beginner!

Jack Nicholson's daughter played Alana with such a natural finesse. Loraine is a charming young actress in front of the camera. She did a great job barfing on the beach just like the real Alana did after the shark attack! Loraine made us cry, but she also made us laugh while she skillfully played Alana with an uncanny likeness. Noah Johnson coached Loraine Nicholson for the more serious role that she had to play.

Sonya (Balmores) Chung is married to Noah's friend Kanoah, who is an avid and talented surfer on Kauai. In real life, Sonya, an excellent surfer, competed against Alana and Bethany in their younger years. Noah was walking by some of the producers in the office and overheard them discussing who could play the part of Malina Birch. They were considering an actress from outside the U.S. when Noah suggested Sonya Chung, a surfer and local Hawaii actress. God has His perfect timing!

Ross Thomas and Chris Brochu, who play our sons, Noah and Tim, were both already natural watermen. They matched our sons' characters perfectly. It was fun watching everyone surf Makaha; and afterward, Chris often entertained us with his guitar and singing.

Kevin Sorbo was matchless in his role! He naturally fit the part of Holt, just like a real hero, and was the perfect surf dad to Alana, Holt's daughter, played by Loraine Nicholson. For his surf lessons, Kevin chose to focus on what he needed to know to look cool and confident on the beach and in the water. He needed to look like an experienced surfer and got tips on detailed aspects of surfing, such as holding his surfboard in a natural manner against a strong wind; how to wax a surfboard like you have been doing it for 35 years; and (this is critical) how to walk across the reef during the rescue scene with very rough waves breaking on the rocks along with an incoming tide! This was one of the toughest scenes to shoot in the whole movie.

Bethany suggested that Jeremy Sumpter, who starred in the 2003 movie *Peter Pan*, play the role of Byron, Holt's son, and the producers agreed. Because of the movie time constraints, his role was limited. The most physically challenging scene in the movie is when Kevin and Jeremy rescue Bethany right after she loses her arm. The camera crew, and even the director, had to live in their wetsuits for days as pounding surf bombarded them. The medic was kept busy with reef cuts and coral implants! Kevin handled it all like a champ.

Arlene Newman-Van Asperen, who plays Sydney, Alana's mother and Holt's wife, is a Hawaii girl from the North Shore of Oahu. Naturally, Arlene fit right into the surf scenes for the movie. She has studied acting for years and won Mrs. Hawaii in 2005. Arlene was my regular prayer partner during the making of *Soul Surfer*. She is gracefully skilled and gifted at Hawaiian dancing. She grew up involved in church, as her father is a minister and her mother a strong prayer warrior. We called her mom a few times to request prayer when we were feeling overwhelmed! Arlene's part was small, but she got to hang out with Kevin Sorbo!

Sarah Hill, Bethany's youth pastor, was hired as a makeup artist. She had met Jesus as her Lord and Savior in Southern California. While surfing a California beach break, she took a bad wipeout and broke her neck and back. God miraculously healed her. Prayer was a strong point in her spiritual life, which is how she received divine direction to move to Hawaii. No one believed her, but she chose to trust God's guidance. She made the move over to Kauai and settled in as a youth leader at North Shore Community Church where we attend. Sarah built friendships with the girls through surfing and Bible study; then the shark attack occurred.

Carrie Underwood landed this key role as youth leader in the film. I believe she fit her role perfectly and had a powerful impact on the outcome of the scene where she spoke the words of Jeremiah 29:11. After going back and forth on whether to keep the verse in the script, the battle ended when Carrie stated that it was a part of the real story and we all should honor the family's wishes.

As believers on the north shore of Kauai, we have fellowshipped and gathered in the name of Jesus at many different locations. Our church has never had our own "home," where you put down solid material roots, housing such tools as a Christian library with loads of great books, DVDs, kids' videos, a prayer chapel, a fine-tuned nursery or an actual building to meet midweek for worship and Bible studies and other gatherings.

Presently we meet under a yellow and green tent with a beautiful shade tree for our prayer chapel.

When the film director Sean McNamara came over to scout out locations for certain scenes, he attended church with us under the tent. But this wasn't where we attend church; it was at Becky's father's church, where he is the worship leader/assistant pastor. Raise your hand if you meet under a tent to worship God! And raise your hand if your son has married a beautiful girl who also meets for worship under another tent! We were on a time crunch and this service fit into the tight schedule. After all, what is the difference between one tent and another? (Visitors must think that here on Kauai we all meet in tents for church services!)

The day we showed up at the beach park for shooting the church tent scene, which I thought was going to be filmed on Kauai but wasn't, I was taken by total surprise. The scene was gloriously beautiful. A white tent was set up on the grass next to the sparkling blue water at a beach park in Kahuku. Tears filled my eyes as I looked on the scene. A large standing wooden cross was set up outside and was included in a scene. And it was so special to watch Timmy work with the camera crew. He has a very amiable personality, and the crew enjoyed working with him. Tom and I, along with some of our friends and some friends and family of other key people, were in the church scene as extras. Imagine that! We got paid to go to church!

Tom and I sat behind Dennis Quaid and Helen Hunt. Then we all sang the special theme song God had given our family right after the shark attack, "Blessed Be Your Name," written by Matt and Beth Redman. We sang it over and over, for take after take after take, but I never got tired of it. We sang it with different angles and slight adjustments, and it was fun, fun, fun!

The funniest part of filming the scene related to our daughter-in-law, Becky, working her job as co-producer. Because Sean McNamara is himself a talented musician, he is great at managing the music scenes. Sean put Becky in charge of keeping us, the worshipers, on track as we sang. Becky's hand stuck out from behind a curtain and went up and down in time with the proper beat as the cameras rolled on us. All we could see was this hand leading worship. It was hilarious! Later, because we spent most of the day filming the tent church scene, the cameras focused on the worship team, which included Becky leading worship along with Carrie Underwood, a friend of Noah's and a girl from San Diego.

The Sunday after Bethany left the hospital after the attack, we all attended church together. For the last song, the worship team played "Blessed Be Your Name," and God totally spoke to me through that song. Some of the words say, "He [God] gives and takes away! Blessed be His name!" We rejoiced together in the truth that no matter what happens in our lives, we are in His hands and He orchestrates our experiences for His divine purposes. This song gave me so much peace. We knew that our heavenly Father was reaching out to us to let us know that He watches over us.

With God's impeccable timing, this song was played in every church service we attended as we traveled during the next year—Australia, New Jersey, England, California, Haleiwa, and many other places. It was a confirmation that we were in His will. At the end of this season, during which I was going through a trial, I asked God to confirm an issue of my heart by playing "Blessed Be Your Name" at church—He did it! I was very surprised and felt very loved by Him.

When the boys were little, I noticed that they had opposite personalities. Timmy had singular focus while Noah had a myriad antennae all tuned in to anything and everything that was going on. Noah's ability to multitask came into play in countless ways in the making of *Soul Surfer*. His tenacious spirit helped him become part of the production team. Heaven provided Becky, our son Noah's wife! She had recently graduated from California State University Fullerton with a degree in filmmaking. Noah and Becky were hired as co-producers to help fine-tune many critical details, some small and others very big. For instance, Noah was a stickler about the clothes that would or would not be worn by surfers portrayed in the movie. They both were involved and made a difference in casting, locations and music. Noah made sure the surfing scenes were kept as authentic as possible.

Except for the few who already knew how to surf, the cast of *Soul Surfer* was schooled on just how difficult it is to balance on a chunk of slick-glassed foam while thousands of pounds of churning water propel you either toward rocks or reef or crashing shorebreak. I know that surfing looks easy; but trust me, compared to almost any other sport, the learning curve for advanced surfing is almost vertical.

You can fast-track your beginner surfing experience with lessons on safety, etiquette and the main surfing skills to minimize your mistakes and possible injuries. It may sound as if no one would want to go back after a challenging day of surf lessons, but the crew of *Soul Surfer* really got with it. Having the right equipment, the right weather and wind conditions, along with perfect beginner waves, one can quickly learn the basics and enjoy riding the warm waves here in Hawaii.

The most important aspect in the film was showcasing Bethany's real surfing abilities, which Noah promoted in Tahiti. Becky was on set every day, advising Sean, our director, about every detail with dialogue, surf lingo and the accuracy of Bethany's portrayal. Noah worked on the water unit team that spent hours filming the competitions. He helped head up and organize the Kauai unit for some of the most dramatic backdrops used in the film. Noah and Becky worked long hours assisting the art department, wardrobe, product placement and stock footage. As one of the set photographers, Noah documented the daily shoots with still photography while Becky videoed the same.

As the filming of *Soul Surfer* progressed, we focused on helping to bring out the real details of the story rather than fiction. There are too many facts in the whole story that are not believable! The entire family, especially Noah and Becky, took great pains to ensure that the film realistically portrayed the surf culture, island life and, of course, our Christian faith. Noah and Becky also rounded up any and all of our Oahu friends to work and be a part of the surf contests or church crowd.

We were especially pleased that Noah was able to get Mike Coots, his friend from surfing, who lived a few houses away from us when we were living in Kilauea, Kauai, involved in the film. Mike had lost his foot to a shark attack in 1998. This occurred while Mike was body boarding on the west side of Kauai with a group of friends who were all highly ranked competitors in the contest arena. He lost the lower part of his leg but survived by fighting the shark off with his bare hands. Like Bethany, Mike didn't let his loss keep him from enjoying the ocean. With the help of a specially designed prosthetic leg, he has learned to stand-up surf along with continuing his passion for body boarding.

Mike went on to get a photography degree at Brooks Institute in Santa Barbara, California. In the film, he plays the part of a photographer shooting Loraine Nicholson, who is playing Alana in the beach photo shoot scene in *Soul Surfer.*

Mike and Bethany's stories are similar: Each was given a choice whether to be defeated or to come back stronger. These days, Mike keeps busy as a professional surf and lifestyle photographer, as well as speaking in defense of sharks from destructive fishing habits such as "finning" (cutting off the fin for food consumption and medical uses, and discarding the rest of the fish, often alive).

Still young, adventurous and full of energy, Mike and another buddy, Miguel, towed the rotting carcass of a wild boar out into the ocean with a jet ski. Miguel waited, finger on the ignition, as Mike lowered a video camera strapped to a long paddle. It wasn't too long before a 16-foot tiger shark appeared and snatched the pig down in one gulp!

There is a lot of down time while scenes are being set up, but everyone seemed to make use of that time to catch up on endless cell phone calls. Sadly, this diminished the opportunity to get to know and interact with others on the set. Turning off all of those phones was critical during each scene take.

With the strong trade winds and saltwater, the hairdressers were at their wits' end. So you won't see your favorite hairdo in *Soul Surfer*! When you're surfing, you don't care how your hair looks. Actually you may care, but there isn't too much you can do about it while getting tossed and turned by the waves. It was an unending task keeping the actors looking like movie stars.

Just being able to have our friends and family involved with us on this amazing project gave us a deeper sense of connection to the incredible fact that a movie was being made about us . . . about how a terrifying event on an October morning didn't destroy us, but instead became a mighty outpouring of unprecedented blessing in our lives and in the lives of others.

A tsunami came to the Hawaiian Islands on February 27, 2010, during the movie production. An 8.8 magnitude earthquake had struck in faraway Chile. Immediately, seismologists warned that a possible 3- to 7-foot tidal wave would race from one end of the Pacific to the other.

Hawaii was right in its path.

Years ago, in the 1950s, our next-door neighbors told us they had lost their oceanfront house in a tsunami but survived by immediately climbing the hill behind their house when they noticed the receding waters in the bay. I realized that tsunamis are something to take seriously. So when the air raid sirens started blaring at 6:00 A.M. on February 27, Sean disrupted our filming schedule and had everyone seek safety. The Turtle Bay Resort had rooms that were three stories high where they recommended the guests, actors and producers retreat.

We stayed put as the phone book tsunami inundation map showed we were high enough on the hill to avoid the surge. We could look out of our window and watch as the neighbors packed up their barbecues, surfboards and jet skis.

We had packed up a car more than once for tsunami alerts in the past. They have all hit but were too small to be of real concern. I researched and knew nothing would endanger us, so we figured this would be an opportunity to catch a few uncrowded waves!

We loaded the car with surfboards and the camera after we saw the report that no tsunami was hitting other Pacific island locations in the path from Chile. The kids had a great surf session until the coast guard helicopter hovered and harassed them to leave the water. I have done intensive research on tsunamis and we have lived through so many false alarms that we were sure this one would have no impact. We have experienced so many really huge surf days that a three-foot surge among the regular waves is not going to keep us up on a hill.

Later, sitting on the beach, I realized that God was showing me a metaphor not only for the film we were making, but also for what has happened in our lives. The event that could have been a tsunami of destruction and fear has turned out to be a wave of blessing. God has always had a plan for us, and He only used the perceived tragedy to advance His plan and embrace the world with a tsunami of love. It was the fulfillment of Jeremiah 29:11 in our lives.

We were in the middle of God's plan and we saw how He was using our lives to draw people to faith in Him. I could see that God has always kept us in His care. He was preparing Tom and me before we even knew Him personally and intimately.

The event that rocked our family didn't send out destruction; it sent out a wave of hope and love in the form of a story of triumph over adversity through our trust in God. The tsunami of God's impact in our lives has not run out of energy. In the telling of our story, people are still being swept off their feet by God's love.

Our journey to this place began long before that shark attacked Bethany. It began far away from the lush tropical beaches of Hawaii. It began with a New Jersey boy in thick square-framed glasses, and an athletic blonde California girl in San Diego.

Notes

1 Laura Sheahen, " 'It's All God': Interview with Dennis Quaid," Beliefnet. http://www.beliefnet.com/Faiths/Christianity/2005/11/Its-All-God-Interview-With-Dennis-Quaid.aspx.

2. "Hilo Hawaii's Noah Johnson Wins the Quicksilver in Memory of Eddie Aikau," HoloHolo Hawai'i, January 1, 1999. http://holoholo.org/quikeddy/q990101.html.

Jersey Boy

*The LORD will fulfill his purpose for me; your love, O LORD,
endures forever—do not abandon the work of your hands.*

PSALM 138:8, *NIV*

Tom was 13 years old when he discovered the joy of surfing.

Does New Jersey strike you as a likely place for a thriving surf culture? News spreads fast and even faster in the surfing world. In August 1888, the cover of a magazine called the *National Police Gazette*, a New Jersey publication, featured a female surfer riding on a wave. This piece of East Coast history is documented by Skipper Funderburg and is part of the Surfing Heritage Foundation collection.

Fast track to 1963, when the Beach Boys had a mega hit song with "Surfing USA." With the help of music, it seemed as if surf fever was catching on everywhere—including the barrier island resort town of Ocean City, New Jersey.

Tom's dad moved the family there from central New Jersey when Tom was a toddler. Tom's dad was a dentist, and I guess he figured he could fix teeth anywhere, so it might as well be close to the beach. So Tom, the youngest, and his two brothers, Mike and Bob, and sister Pat, found themselves in quaint and family friendly Ocean City, a small town of around 8,000 people that swelled in number every summer. When summer rolled around, Ocean City's famous boardwalks were crowded to bursting with a great view of friendly, rideable waves.

During that summer of 1963, the only thing that mattered to Tom and his best friend, Monk, were the waves peeling across the water off the jam-packed beach—waves that suddenly had a new meaning: Surfing!

For most Americans, surfing was just another novelty fad like the hula-hoop or 3D movies. Surfers were daredevils riding monstrous waves in Hawaii, or hanging 10 in bikini-clad California—both faraway places from Tom and Monk's everyday world.

With his strong swimming background, it was a natural course of events that Tom found something to pursue outside of the pool. Of all his siblings, he was the rowdy one, the restless one, the "Trickster," as his surf crew named him. His nickname came not because he was mischievous, although that was true as well, but because he could do some tricky things with a pool stick.

Tom got booted out of parochial school for pelting one of the sisters with an eraser. You can imagine that his good Irish Catholic parents might have thought they had their hands full with their fourth child, especially since they only meant to have three children.

Tom's parents were steadfast, and like many in their generation, they made sure everyone was off to Mass each Sunday. It was more than just what they did; it was part of who they were as a classic Irish Catholic family.

As much trouble as Tom caused the poor nuns, and for all his complaining about those boring church services, if you asked my husband about it now, Tom knew that the seeds of the gospel were planted in his heart because of the consistency and devotion his parents demonstrated in their faith.

Church wasn't the only activity that was important to them. The Hamiltons were an athletic family, and the ocean was a big part of their life. They were all strong swimmers, including Tom's mother. His parents actually met in a swimming pool on an ocean liner going to Ireland. Each was in college and already engaged to another but fell in love—hook, line and sinker—on the Atlantic Ocean. Tom's brother Mike received swim scholarships and became a teacher at Atlantic City High School. He also became the school's swim coach, and he was a lifeguard at the beach every summer until his retirement.

Like his brother, Tom also was a swimmer throughout high school, but it was surfing that truly grabbed his heart and soul. Right there at the end of Ocean City High School, across the crowded boardwalk, clean rideable waves came racing out of the Atlantic to curl along the sand bar next to the Music Pier. If you wanted to surf, you needed to have the right equipment to enjoy riding the waves.

With youthful determination, Tom's best friend, Monk, got his hands on a surfboard. The '60s era surfboards, or tankers, as they were nicknamed, were clunky, oversized boards and weighed almost as much as your typical 13-year-old. The board was too heavy to carry alone.

The waves kept enticing from the end of the boardwalk, but there was no way that Monk could haul the board down to the beach. It might as well have been across the country. So the two boys came up with a plan. They would share the board and carry it together to and from the beach.

All that summer the two of them could be seen lugging around that giant board, Tom clutching the nose and Monk the tail, as they made their way across town. They learned to surf in shifts, taking turns on the one board they had between them. There was another serious hurdle Tom had to overcome in order to improve in his surfing. He was (and still is) very near-sighted—so much so that he wore thick black-rimmed glasses, not something you can wear in the saltwater and breaking waves. Without glasses, he was lost and disoriented in the water. Tom could not see the waves coming until they were right on top of him.

So Tom learned to rely on the feel of the water as it shifted and to anticipate the movement of other surfers around him. He knew that when everyone else suddenly paddled off toward the horizon, a set of waves was coming in. He learned to surf in an instinctively sensitive technique.

Years later, in Hawaii, Tom had his late takeoffs wired. He was known for surfing one particularly harrowing surf spot—a reef break where he'd drop into the waves with wild abandon, taking off at the last second. I said something about how crazy he was to take such late hairy drops, as if he lived for thrills. Usually, when surfers see a big set coming, everyone paddles hard to pick up speed to drop into a wave. If it is too late to drop in, you can have a very nasty wipeout, especially when the waves have some size. Tom confessed to me that his bravado came from his poor eyesight. He could never really see just how late his takeoff was, so he perfected his instincts and learned to drop into the biggest and gnarliest waves somewhat blindly. Amazingly, he made the drop most of the time.

Ocean City, New Jersey, in the summer of 1963, was the watershed for Tom. He and Monk immersed themselves in the small world of New Jersey surfing. By Labor Day, the boardwalk shut down after a summer of activity. The stores, the many eateries, the amusement parks along the boardwalk, the miniature golf parks all closed down for the winter and the Shoe-bees (a slang term for the summer-time visitors, who brought their lunch in a shoe box) crawled back home in the end of summer traffic. By the time school opened, Tom and Monk were fairly proficient and completely hooked on surfing.

With the hint of coming winter in the air, the boys surfed after school and on weekends, knowing their time was running out before the winter snows fell. They went out as soon as dawn made the waves visible and until the setting sun had faded into darkness. Neither of the boys had a wetsuit, so when the weather started to turn, eventually it became just too cold to surf. Reluctantly, they put the surfboard into hibernation up in the garage rafters.

It must have felt like the longest winter ever before the new year thawed and the weather warmed enough to get back into the water. For his birthday, Tom's father bought him his first surfboard. He got it at the local hardware store, and in spite of the Hawaiian name and fancy logo, it was an authentic "pop out" board—a cheap mass-manufactured surfboard. Tom didn't care; it was his!

Tom's dad later admitted to him that he almost regretted ever buying him that board. "That's the moment I lost you," he would say. The sport of surfing, not family, school or church, became the driving force in Tom's life from that moment on.

That first summer went by in a flash of surf, surf and more surf. Both Tom and Monk quickly learned to check the buoys and scour the weather reports for swells generated by hurricanes and tropical storms moving up the Atlantic. But even without the bigger, faster waves generated by these storms, there were plenty of good fun waves to be had on the shifting sandbars along the coast. As the warm days drew to a close, the boys knew they had to find a way to surf all year round.

We're still talking about New Jersey here . . . in the winter. Tom tells our kids, who are spoiled by the year-round warmth of the tropics, wild stories about coming out of the ocean with icicles forming on his hair and eyebrows and having fingers so numb that he had to ask strangers to put the key in the car door lock.

Of course, our children can't relate to what he is saying at all.

Somehow, both Tom and Monk scrounged up enough money for wetsuits. These weren't the nice, flexible wetsuits we have in today's surf shops; back in the early sixties, those things were crude, clunky and expensive. They were made for diving, not surfing, and were beyond uncomfortable.

Tom and Monk had to grease their armpits with Vaseline to avoid getting a chafing rash from the rigid neoprene as they paddled. Then there was the whole buttoning, yanking, tugging on of the whole contraption, including a ridiculous-looking beaver tail that was supposed to keep icy water from rushing up into the jacket. And then top off the whole affair with booties, gloves and a hood that would barely let you turn your head. They had to work hard to enjoy the winter swells.

With the stores along the boardwalk shuttered until spring, and the amusement rides closed down, the sight of two young boys waddling through the snow in those seal suits, surfboards balanced on their heads, must have been a bizarre sight to the few year-round Ocean City residents. With stiff movements because of the wetsuits, and chilled to the bone, the boys would surf in the freezing water until they could no longer endure it.

But was it ever worth it! If the beaches and waves were crowded during the summer, the surfing population of Ocean City shrank dramatically in the winter. No more than a few dozen surfers were part of the hard-core crew that surfed year round in these adventurous conditions. By the time spring rolled around, these daring young surfers celebrated its return and their survival with a Polar Bear surf contest.

Like all young surfers, when the surf was flat, Tom spent idle hours hanging out at the local surf shop. Eventually, George, the owner, asked him if he wanted a job. Thinking of how he'd be able to afford his own custom-made surfboard to replace his beat-up old pop-out, Tom agreed. He was a fast learner, and soon George taught him the art of repairing surfboards.

With the summer crowds, it was inevitable that surfers would crash their boards into each other, into the pier or into some hardheaded tourist who swam out too far. Then there were all the guys who were a little too careless in tying their boards down on car roof racks. Step on the gas and—*whoop!*—board goes flying off. It didn't matter if you were part of the hard-core crew or a weekend warrior, eventually you'd ding up your board.

Soon, as business picked up, repairing surfboards became the only thing Tom did for the surf shop. Because he had been well trained, Tom could speed through the work of the day and still have lots of time to surf. And because he now had a job, he was finally able to purchase his own custom surfboard. Even to this day, when traveling with Bethany in the professional surfing circuit, it's not uncommon for Tom to turn their hotel room into a repair shop stacked with boards awaiting his attention.

When not surfing, Tom and his surf buddies spent hours poring over the surfing magazines that featured crisp blue waves towering over the iconic surfers of the day. Those waves didn't resemble anything off the New Jersey beaches, not even on those big days when violent storms in the Arctic Circle created perfect icy tubes to tempt surfers across the snowy sand for a quick barrel and an instant ice-cream headache.

No, the waves in those magazines were on distant shores: California, Hawaii, Mexico. Tom dreamed about paddling into waves like that. All he asked his parents for, over and over, was a surf trip across the country to California. For his graduation gift, in the summer of 1968, Tom got his wish. He was 18 years old, and it was his first time on an airplane; but that new thrill paled in comparison to the fact that he was finally going to surf in the Pacific Ocean.

Tom, my future husband, flew into California with visions of a surfing paradise, but his visions paled in comparison to the wonderful land of Southern California that greeted him.

The palm trees, the miles of coast, the endless waves, the girls . . . it was like he'd died and gone to heaven. Everywhere he turned there was a famous surf spot, and the waves themselves! They didn't look like this back where he came from.

Tom ended up in Hermosa Beach, California, in the South Bay area of the Los Angeles basin. For a few wonderful weeks he prowled up and down the Pacific Coast Highway hitting surf spot after surf spot, from sunup to sundown. Then, tanned, satiated, yet already dreaming of his next surf trip, Tom flew back home to New Jersey.

A surprise awaited him in the mailbox, one that would change his life forever.

A draft notice.

Ticket to 'Nam

*Trust in the LORD with all your heart and lean not
to your own understanding; in all your ways acknowledge
him, and he will make your paths straight.*

PROVERBS 3:5-6, *NIV*

When Lee Harvey Oswald pulled the trigger on that fateful day in Dallas, in November 1963, Vice President Lyndon B. Johnson inherited the Oval Office and a war. The conflict that became the Vietnam War had been building since World War II. By the time John F. Kennedy was assassinated, it was rapidly escalating.

For most Americans, the tension in Southeast Asia was a distant annoyance that took a backseat to what was happening in Cuba and the arms-and-space-race with Russia. But what seemed only to be a slow cooking "police action" began heating up under LBJ as more Americans were shipped overseas, and more were sent back in flag-draped boxes.

More than any other war or conflict since the U.S. Civil War, Vietnam divided America. The politics, the protests . . . the fabric of the nation that had been woven so tightly by the preceding generations was suddenly coming unraveled.

By 1968, the country was in turmoil over the policies that spawned the war, over the point of the war and its cost, and there was an ever-deepening mistrust in the government. It seemed like every person under 30 was busy squaring off in rowdy and, sometimes, violent confrontation against anyone seen as "The Establishment."

It was a time of counterculture and conflicting ideology. People questioned what it meant to be a patriot; they questioned America's purpose. I was in the sixth grade when, one day after school, I answered a knock at the door. There I saw two men in black, complete with government-issue sunglasses. The men identified themselves with their FBI badges and asked to see my father. He was home for the day after teaching American history, and the agents informed him that he was to not talk negatively to his students about America's involvement in Vietnam.

Tom has always told me that he was oblivious to any of this. His whole world was surfing—a world far removed from politics, protests, wars and all its horrors. Perhaps he was unusual for a young man of his generation, but Tom thought, talked and dreamed of nothing but surfing.

So it was with dread that he pulled the slim, official-looking letter out of his mailbox. The words "selective service" above a notification to present himself to the United States military induction center in Philadelphia for a physical suddenly brought that wider world rushing in upon him.

Tom's friends told him not to worry; the Army doctors would most likely reject him. Not only did he have bad eyes, flat feet and a hammertoe (which made wearing military boots and hiking for long periods of time unfeasible), but like other surfers of that era, he also had "surfer's knots" on his knees and feet. These were large, protruding calcium deposits that developed as a result of extended kneeling on a hard surface. (Even the apostle James was nicknamed "old camel knees" by the Early Church because he reputedly spent so much time on his knees in prayer!)

Before shortboards, surfers used to paddle on their knees, with their feet tucked up underneath them. Today's surfers lie prone because the small size of surfboards do not facilitate knee paddling. Back then, those knots were an insider's mark of dedication to surfing. And they were also usually a ticket out of military service.

Most Army doctors had never seen a surf knot, and so the first batch of surfers to show up for an induction physical were stamped 4-F—physically unfit for military service. Of course, most of the surfers appreciated the irony of being rejected, and certainly they weren't letting on that this mysterious affliction that marred an otherwise fit and athletic-looking man would shrink harmlessly away after a few months off the surfboard.

Bolstered by these assertions of a 4-F stamp, Tom waited for the date of his physical and drove the 70 miles to Philadelphia. The induction center was jammed with guys like him, all 18 to 20 years old. Tom filled out a few forms and was ushered into a room where he was given a multiple-page test that started with a basic problem such as drawing a line from the picture of a screwdriver to the object that matched it; nut, nail or screw.

Of course, whole rows of guys intentionally answered every question wrong, thus guaranteeing themselves a position in the infantry. Tom answered the questions honestly, trusting in his 4-F knees, feet and eyesight. After the test, Tom was conducted to a locker room where everything he had on besides his undies were stripped off and stashed away. Paperwork in hand, he was told to follow the white line to the physical evaluation station. Tom looked down at his knotty knees and gnarled feet and trudged along without complaining.

What he didn't know was how great the military's appetite for new troops had grown and that the acceptable physical standards were dropping rapidly. Tom passed the physical with flying colors and was told he had three months of freedom before he belonged wholly and irrevocably to the United States Armed Forces.

Right about then, Tom paid attention to the war his nation was wrestling with. As his time on the outside dwindled, he dreaded being stuck crawling neck-deep in jungle mud as a grunt—avoiding land mines, snipers, booby traps; lying in foxholes; catching malaria. You name it—he knew he didn't want any part of it.

Tom's swim coach turned out to be a commander in the Navy Reserves, and he graciously used his connections to help Tom get an enlistment into the Navy. This is an example of when "who you know" counts at a turning point in your life.

At the end of his three months, he reported to Lakehurst Naval Air Station in New Jersey, for boot camp, and boy did he get a rude awakening.

The life of a surfer has its own sort of regimentation, its own discipline and endurance. But the military regimentation, discipline and tests of endurance are a far cry from the self-imposed life of a dedicated surfer. Being yelled at by drill sergeants; called every name in the book and all the ones not in the book; being forced to march, stand, wake, eat, dig holes, fill holes, at any time, with no seeming rhyme or reason—all were a bit of an adjustment for Tom. He still laughs about being "leader of the pack" to do punitive pushups.

Boot camp spit him out, and soon after, Tom got his orders. Only four months after his California Dreamin' surf trip, Tom found himself heading back to California, to North Island Naval Station in San Diego, where he was assigned to the Navy destroyer *USS Hanson*.

Because he could type well, Tom ended up with the opportunity to work in and be in charge of the ship's post office—a particularly enviable job in the days before electronic media, because a letter or package from home was the only way that family and friends could communicate with their loved ones at sea. The postmaster was appreciated by the crew, so much so that Tom was often given little gifts by happy sailors out of the care packages he delivered—homemade cookies, dried fruit and then some.

While most of the time the ship's postman was treated like a good fellow by most of the crew, there was one petty officer who resented the fact that Tom, a wet-behind-the-ears kid, had pulled such light duty. He took every chance to harass Tom until one day it came to a head. The two men found themselves in a "smoker"—an officially sanctioned boxing match where enlisted men could settle their grievances by pure force.

The officer was bigger and more experienced than Tom, but Tom's father was a true fighting Irishman who'd won many bouts in his youth, including a national championship at age 12. He passed on a few of his fatherly fighting tips to his son, and after years of surfing, Tom was in better shape. He eventually knocked the other guy down and finished the fight. But that only made things worse. Ego bruised, the officer's grudge burned fiercer.

Tom decided that there was a better way to fight back, and since direct action hadn't worked, this time he'd try something non-confrontational but effective. Every time the mail came in for Tom to sort, he quietly hid anything destined for the petty officer in the ship's safe—which only he and the captain had access to.

Every mail call, the officer watched as everyone else got letters and packages from home while he got nothing. The officer couldn't understand it; his wife wrote him regularly, even numbering the letters.

Tom could see the suspicion and frustration building. The guy knew something was up, but he couldn't prove anything. Four mail calls later, Tom handed the officer a huge packet of numbered mail wrapped in rubber bands. Tom never gloated or threatened, but from that moment on the harassment ended.

For a while, Tom and the *USS Hanson* patrolled on standby along the California coast. The crew was kept busy with menial tasks of sanding, painting and scrubbing. While the Vietnam War raged on, and the nation fractured over it, it looked like they wouldn't be deployed. When the call came down, they had only three days' notice before getting underway for the Gulf of Tonkin and war.

But war was still distant in Tom's mind. He enjoyed being out on the open ocean and would often escape the sights, sounds and smells of seasick crewmen below deck by climbing the signalman's bridge to stand in the open air and watch waves bowl over the bow of the ship during storms.

Love of the ocean kept him up there even when it meant getting thoroughly soaked. And the deep, rolling Pacific, miles from shore, fed his soul. He would look out across the expanse of never-ending blue and think of perfect waves peeling along some hidden coast.

Tom had already figured out who the surfers were aboard the *Hanson* because of the surf magazines coming to them through the mail. One of them was a young body surfer named Rob, who hailed from Oahu. Rob was always talking about the brutal shore break at Makapu'u, or about how much better the waves were in Hawaii than anywhere else.

"You should surf some *real* waves!" he would kid Tom, "Not those itty-bitty-kiddie waves they have in California or the East Coast." Instead of being goaded to defend his home breaks, Tom recalled the pictures splashed across every other page in the surfing magazines, showing Hawaii as a surf Mecca, a tropical feast of nonstop perfect waves.

You can imagine how excited Tom was in knowing that the first port of call was Pearl Harbor. At last he'd made it to Hawaii, though arriving by Navy destroyer was not the way he'd imagined. Tom couldn't wait to get off the ship. It was only a short stop, but Tom and some of the others managed to surf Waikiki. It was Tom's first experience with the warm Hawaiian waves.

"And just think, if you moved to Hawaii you would never have to wear a wetsuit again!" Rob told him with a grin.

He had no idea just how appealing this was to Tom.

But the day drew to a close and they had to report back to the ship. In the morning, they sailed out of the peaceful fiftieth state and toward war.

There were a few other ports of call, and though Tom had never been out of the country, unlike a lot of the men on his ship, he was not particularly enchanted with the seedy rows of flesh dens, grimy bars and alleys full of con artists aggressively trying to hustle any sailor they could. In particular, he remembers Subic Bay in the Philippines as inciting both pity and revulsion for the desperation with which people hounded the sailors—offering everything, including themselves, for money or cigarettes or trinkets.

Not to mention that Tom recalls that sick bay was always full after the more infamous ports.

From Subic Bay, Tom's ship escorted the aircraft carrier *Kitty Hawk* to Vietnam, where they anchored a mile offshore, providing fire support for the marines and army onshore.

The blast of the huge guns spewing explosive shells deep into the jungle was exhilarating at first, but when Tom started to listen in on the accuracy reports, he was faced with war in a way that conflicted and disturbed him. Over the headset, he heard artillery spotters report that the shells had missed their mark and landed on a village of "friendlies." Tom sat in silence, trying not to imagine the innocent men, women and children snuffed out by his ship's guns. He tried to dismiss them as collateral damage, like the guy on the radio did, but it haunted him.

Still, he had an enviably safe job, miles offshore, far from the brutal field conditions and persistent violence and horrors of war. Sometimes he got to head into the nearby base via helicopter, on a "milk run," ferrying bags of mail to and from the ship. But overall, his war experience was cushy. The things that happened in the wet jungles couldn't touch him.

Tom's nonchalant sense of security came to an end during a standard milk run over a dense rain forest that was supposed to be enemy-free.

The Vietnam War had come for Tom.

To this day, Tom won't talk about it. So I let what happened remain in obscurity. Maybe someday he'll be ready to talk about it, or maybe not. I can respect that he doesn't want to ever revisit his experience.

But I do believe that the shock of "this can't be happening to me!" that Tom got that day in Vietnam was a kind of preparation, or maybe a dress rehearsal, for the similar dismantling of our own nest of casual security when we first heard that our daughter, Bethany, had been viciously mauled by the second most dangerous shark in the world.

Vietnam could be blamed on politicians and revolutionaries. In the case of Bethany, when Tom wrestled with the very real possibility of losing his daughter forever, there seemed to be only one person to blame . . . God.

CHAPTER

4

Destiny

My times are in your hands.

PSALM 31:15, *NIV*

My dad was born in Denver, Colorado, and he lived his life with a high level of activity and adventure. I can get dizzy watching the home movies my mother took in the early years of their marriage.

In high school, he was a super athlete and achieved a high level of skill in most sports. His abilities are showcased in back-to-back clips of skiing, gymnastics, tennis, high dive and swimming laps—including the breaststroke, butterfly and crawl. He is shown horseback riding, ice-skating, cross-country skiing, and more.

After high school, he joined the Marines and was recruited to play on their football team. His team won the annual United States Football Championship two years in a row at Quantico, Virginia, against the Army! After his military commitment, he was able to go to college on the G.I. bill, in Denver. He studied and worked hard to make it on his own, while barely surviving on peanut butter and crackers.

In his last year of college, my parents met on a double date, although they were not paired with each other. My mom was attracted right off and nabbed a date with him soon after, followed by marriage and the birth of my older sister, Debbie. After completing his four-year degree at Denver University, my dad landed his first teaching job in a nearby mountain town called Glenwood Springs. Dad and Mom packed up my one-year-old sister, Debbie, and Grandma Julia, and moved to their new home.

Glenwood Springs was not only my birthplace, but also the place where I first fell in love with water. In Glenwood, hot volcanic mineral springs bubble up to fill what was the largest swimming pool in the world back in 1953. This premier pool was the first training ground for two future surfer girls. The pool stays open all year round, even in the dead of winter when you can immerse your tired muscles and achy bones into these naturally hot, healing waters under glittering snowfall or a starry summer night.

My dad took his first position teaching history and coaching the wrestling team. This meant traveling on weekends to various high school competitions. Late one night, while my dad was away at a competition, my mom went into labor. Without a car, she left my sister asleep in the crib while she, accompanied by Grandma Julia, carefully walked over icy sidewalks in the falling snow to the small hospital clinic. It was 4:00 A.M. on Valentine's Day, 1953, when I came into the world, ready to fall in love with the water and begin training to live my ocean-bound life.

My parents were probably the most regular swimmers at the hot springs pool. We have photos of my sister and me jumping into the pool as babies. It must have been easy to become water babies where the land is covered with several feet of freezing snow and the pool water is warm and wonderful!

After two years in snowy Glenwood Springs, my dad took a new job in the dusty, dry desert of Arizona, at Yuma High School. We found a house in a family neighborhood with lots of desert critters. We missed the hot springs pool back in the mountains of Colorado, so my mom came to our rescue. She had our backyard paradise fenced in to keep out the rattlesnakes, and then she made a water park playground to cool us off. We turned brown from playing in our kiddie pool under the blazing Arizona sun.

My younger sister, Karin, soon arrived. When she got big enough, she was put in charge of squirting us with the hose. My mom kept busy washing diapers, which were completely dry by the time she hung the last one up. This was a big change from the frozen diapers hanging stiffly on the line in Glenwood Springs! My mother took great care of us. She sewed beautiful little dresses for Easter, enrolled us in ballet dance classes, curled our hair and made the best taquitos ever! My dad, though, was California dreaming. He worked extra after-school hours selling cars to save up vacation money to scout out San Diego.

During the summer break, our family would pack up our station wagon and go camping on just about every beach in California. We went everywhere along the ocean, which helped my dad confirm his decision to move to San Diego. He loved the beaches, the zoo, the beautiful harbor; and he set his course to eventually move to this wonderful beach-lined city. It wasn't long before his winning reputation as a wrestling coach at Yuma High caught the notice of a football coach at San Diego High. I once asked him about his two state championship victories in Yuma. He said the real secret to his success was the amazing talent of his team who were mostly Navaho indigenous people.

At last, our ocean-bound destiny became a reality. We packed up our Ford Fairlane station wagon and moved to San Diego.

You might get the impression that my parents liked to move around a lot. But the truth is, once they got to San Diego, California, that was it. Looking back, I can only thank God.

Like Tom, my family ended up living near the beach. But you can hardly get any farther removed from New Jersey beaches than sunny Southern California, where I grew up. Once I hit elementary school, I was firmly ensconced in the idyllic fifties-era childhood—Barbie dolls, roller skates (they had steel wheels back then), and Saturday movie matinees, complete with Giant Sweet Tarts, Milk Duds and sticky floors.

Today, with all the dangers to children that we see in the news, it's hard to imagine a time when the only real rule was to be back home by the time the street lights turned on.

We had a limited spiritual education as children. My mother would take us to church on Christmas and Easter—like most people. Because we had just moved to San Diego, and we didn't have any friends yet, Sunday School would be a great way to meet some other neighborhood children. We'd walk to a nearby church, probably to enjoy wearing our pretty homemade dresses of frilly taffeta and our white gloves. It was only when, one Sunday, I happened to pick a rose growing over the fence of a house along the way to church that everything went wrong.

He must have been deranged, because some old man came rushing out of the house, swearing and yelling at us. He swung a shining butcher knife over his head. We didn't stay to see if he was crazy enough to use it; but because of that terrifying experience, we stayed home on Sundays from then on, and that stunted my spiritual education. Occasionally, our folks would take us to a beach area church that was having Vacation Bible School so they could have a few hours on the sand without us.

Once we were all in school, my mom went to night school and took classes to complete her teaching credential. This allowed my mom and dad to share vacation times with the family. I also remember that they would use us as guinea pigs for all the different kinds of educational and intelligence tests their schools were experimenting with.

Please don't get the impression that I was a dainty china doll. Sure, we had music lessons (piano lessons, and I even played violin in the school orchestra), and we played dress-up; but Dad made us do yard work with push mowers, and my sisters and I rode bikes, played kickball, explored canyons and romped all over half a dozen beaches. Surfing wasn't on my horizon yet, but I can only imagine that many people viewed it as just another fad that would fade away. Playing with jacks would be all the rage when, suddenly, for no particular reason, hopscotch took over to be followed by marbles and then foursquare.

Our whole family was the outdoorsy type. Dad would load us all up with the tent in our station wagon (the minivan of the time), and we'd spend summer vacations camping along the Pacific coastline, all the way north into Oregon.

My dad was a hard-working guy, always having to be doing something. He worked a side job at a local hotel; and on top of that, he attended college for his master's degree. He'd decorate the yard with tiki torches and turned our front porch into a tropical garden. He also bought beat-up homes near the beach, and we would spend weekends helping to fix them up for resale. Then my sisters and I could take our canvas air-mattress rafts and play around in the ocean.

The beaches became our new playground as we fine-tuned our water skills on rubber rafts, riding waves all summer long. My parents soon found their favorite beach at La Jolla Cove. It was a snorkeling wonderland. We swam alongside my dad as we held our spears in readiness. I don't remember ever catching a fish by myself, because I couldn't bear the thought of killing one.

We learned to get abalone and let my dad get the lobsters. It was painful to watch them die as they were dropped into the boiling water when we returned home for dinner.

The Gidget scene (remember those beach movies?) was exploding in Los Angeles. Our cousins, who lived in West Covina, were very aware of this latest surfing craze. My mom's brother, who was an officer for the LAPD (Los Angeles Police Department), had four daughters. His oldest daughter, Kathy, was now sweet 16, and she decided that she wanted to try surfing. She figured that as soon as her family planned a visit to her water-immersed cousins down in San Diego, she would plan a surf venture.

My sister Debbie and I agreed to rent two boards and give surfing a try. My mom dropped us off at the Gordon and Smith Surf Shop in Mission Beach, a tiny hole in the wall, and we rented two boards for 50 cents each per hour. With the sidewalk baking our feet, we three girls took turns doubling up, carrying the heavy surfboards for a 20-minute walk up Mission Beach Drive to the designated surf zone. That left 20 minutes to surf before we had to walk back another 20 minutes to the surf shop, completing our one-hour rental.

Debbie and Kathy rode their first waves as I watched from the shore. Then, at last, it was my turn. I took hold of the board and pushed it out just inside the main middle breaking section of waves. I knew I didn't have much time left before we had to return, so I just went for it and took off on a little ankle snapper wave barely six inches high. When I reached the shore, I was told it was time to go back; so taking turns carrying the heavy boards, we walked back silently, inwardly focused on our thrilling adventure. I was so elated! Although I had only caught one tiny wave, I knew even then that this was all I ever wanted to do. All of my other goals in life disappeared: all of my plans for the future—being a P.E. coach, my art, all of my other sports. All I could think of was surfing and how I could go out again.

Debbie and I pooled our savings and bought a yellow Gordon and Smith longboard for $30. Not too long after, we each had our own surfboard and were paddling out into the lineup at Law Street in Pacific Beach. We learned to surf by trial and error. Our first big error was trying to surf after covering our bodies with baby oil, which was the tanning rage of the day. It took us a few embarrassing days of constantly slipping off of our boards before the light went on! We became part of a small minority of avid surfer girls in a male-dominated world.

Debbie and I soon had surf knots on our knees and the tops of our feet. We rode 9-foot-6-inch, 30-pound long boards, or tankers, as they were nicknamed. They were heavy, which is probably the main reason most girls did not take up surfing. At first, we would both carry a surfboard to the water; but soon the guy surfers at Law Street would always insist on helping us out and even waxing them for us with the standard paraffin wax. Everyone always shared wax back then, as it was cheap!

We hung out with the same group of guys at the beach all summer long. Most of them were excellent surfers who only really cared about riding the waves. We always saw Skip Fry and enjoyed watching his amazing style. Not every girl could handle it. In the late sixties, surfboards were still big and heavy. Leashes hadn't even been invented yet; so if you wiped out, it meant a long swim in chilly water to get your board back. Wetsuits made specifically for surfing were in their infancy and were largely ineffective. While conditions were nothing like what Tom was experiencing back in New Jersey, a cold February morning in the kelp-filled Pacific could turn you blue and numb in a hurry. It made sense that most people considered surfing to be a sport only for tough, hardy males. Someone forgot to tell my sister and me. Even if they had, we would have paddled back out for more.

We improved our surfing pretty fast, but Debbie was always the best. She could switch stance so naturally and had the most amazingly smooth style going for the biggest of the set waves! We had fun paddling out on our knees and would stand up when going over an unbroken wave. Otherwise, it was a workout to plow through the wave with a push up when trying to get out past the breaking surf.

We didn't have leashes back in the 1960s, so we had to keep our guard up and not get hit by a flying board after someone wiped out. I began to surf well by most standards for women, and I won several contests back then, but I always felt second because of my sister's incredible talent.

One day, my parents would not let us bring our surfboards to the beach because the surf was supposed to get really big. We were so upset when we got to the beach, because the surf was perfect, with nice shoulder-high waves just like we liked it.

Once in a while, our family would go to Ocean Beach, and we would surf by the jetties, but my parents preferred to go to La Jolla Cove. They would drop us off at Law Street to surf because it was on the way to their beach. An unusual coincidence was that two other girls, named Debbie and Shary Melville, the same ages as we were, surfed the same break! Later in life, I found out that Debbie Melville got married on the same day as Tom and I did. Not to mention that my co-author, Rick Bundschuh, surfed Law Street at the same time and was best friends with my boyfriend!

After my older sister got her driver's license, we could get to the beach on our own. We borrowed my mom's car and started surfing Sunset Cliffs regularly. We liked the reefs, as it was an easier paddle out through a channel, not having to punch through closed-out sets at the beach breaks.

We damaged Mom's car several times and busted out the oil pan going over the bumpy dirt road at the end of Sunset Cliffs. Then we wrecked her driver's car door when we pushed the car out of the garage with the car door open in order to not wake up our parents at 5:00 A.M. But I don't ever remember my mom getting mad at us!

Soon my sister got a boyfriend, and I was surfing by myself. Abandoned, I started hitchhiking with my surfboard to the beach. At 16, I got my driver's license, and my dad bought me a car, so I didn't have to hitchhike anymore. He probably saved my life!

After I got a car, I would surf Sunset Cliffs every day at Abs. I surfed it for a solid six years. On occasion, I would go north up to the Cardiff area and surf Pipes. In high school, I made friends who surfed, and we would all pitch in for gas to go surfing. My friend, Pam Falgren, from high school tennis, also surfed. And she always made everything extra fun.

Not only were my parents teachers, but they were also history buffs. It was popular in the sixties to put murals on your walls, so we had the Greek Parthenon painted on our living room walls and marble furniture that looked like it came from Greece. Our specialty home deco was a statue in the living room of Venus de Milo almost two feet tall. This is one of the most famous sculptures of ancient Greece. How many kids grow up with that in their living room? I now see it as God preparing my eyes for what the future would hold.

After the shark attack, we had a week of interviews at a friend's house up in Kalihiwai Ridge. As soon as I walked into the living room, I was confronted with the Venus de Milo statue again! It was too close to home. No one else noticed it until I pointed it out. But it reminded me that I had grown up with that statue.

Later, when Bethany and I attended the ESPY Awards in Hollywood and stayed at the Morovian Hotel on Sunset Blvd, I noticed that our hotel room contained old antique items that were for sale, and our room had a magazine with the Venus de Milo statue featured on the cover. It was a bit strange to have this recurring theme.

Bethany eventually made it to Paris and got a photo in the Louvre Museum of the real thing!

There was a time when I was in love with Jesus. It was in those halcyon days when my parents would drop us off at Vacation Bible School. The church was known as Emmanuel Baptist Church, and it was one of the early hot zones of what people now call "The Jesus Movement."

Whatever label you give it, back then Emmanuel was an interesting intersection of imaginative and welcoming youth ministry that made a group of surfers, hippie types and kids on the edge of culture feel loved while sharing with them the message of Christ in a way they understood.

Even as a child, I had a hunger for truth. Both my parents were educators, so I guess it was natural that I would enjoy learning. But this was a deeper sort of learning, not just rules of grammar or memorization of facts. I resonated with the simple message of the love of God. So, at the end of summer, I entered elementary school in love with Jesus. I felt a peace in knowing that He was God and that He loved me. I knew that He would hear me if I called out to Him.

But I was alone in my faith. After that beautiful summer at Emmanuel, there was no one close to me to encourage me on my spiritual journey, no one to teach me or introduce me to the principles of Christ or a better understanding of God. Except for the short-lived Sunday School excursion, my faith was isolated.

And then it began to wilt.

I was wheeling around town when I decided to stop by the local thrift store to look for castaway treasure. I picked up a book for a dime that told a true story about a sickly kid who was nursed back to health and won a swimming championship. The author wasn't trying to preach Christianity; it wasn't even a Christian book, nor was the book about God at all. The author simply stated that health was built up by cooperating with the God-ordained complexity of the human body via good nutrition.

It planted the seed of the idea that maybe we aren't just accidents of nature, that someone designed us for a purpose, that maybe there could possibly, perhaps, be something—Someone—beyond us, namely, God. I realized that this open door to the possible existence of God meant that I wasn't an atheist anymore, but an agnostic.

I know this isn't much of a step, but if C. S. Lewis was right, at least it was going in the right direction. As funny as it might sound, I was quite proud to be an agnostic. It made me feel much more intellectual and tolerant than being an atheist. The position of "maybe" is far less totalitarian than "impossible." As a teenager in the sixties, without a moral compass, I was bombarded with "opportunities" that demanded much more wisdom than I had the skill to navigate.

The drug culture had swept in and overwhelmed many in the surf culture. Looking back now, it seems incredible that as particular as we were about keeping our physical health in prime condition, most of my friends didn't view pot use as a problem. I am sad to say that far too many incredible and gifted surfers were swept away from the ocean and the sport they loved.

But I was young, and I pretty much went along with whatever my group was doing, which usually meant playing around with drugs (mostly pot) whenever there was a lull in the surfing activity. And being one of the few girls in the company of a lot of boys, it was inevitable that I'd get involved with them at a very young age.

I started going out with one of them—Tony was his name—when I was 16. He was an exceptional surfer and board maker. Immediately after graduating high school, I moved in with him and started college.

Even then, God was calling me to remember Him. I just wasn't that interested in listening. I know that a good number of surfers were coming to faith in Christ during this time, including the popular artist Rick Griffin, whose (now) Christian-tinged work was everywhere in *Surfer* magazine. Somehow none of this caught my attention even though I read *Surfer* avidly.

And then there was my friend Pamela. Pam became a Christian during our senior year, and our relationship changed. She'd been my close friend and tennis partner, but now all she wanted to do was talk about God and Jesus. Looking back, I see how patient and gentle she was, even though I was somewhat derisive of her enthusiasm and beliefs. I know now the heartache she must have felt for me. She was so excited about what the Lord had done in her life; but any time she tried to share it with me, I flat-out told her I wasn't interested in hanging out with "Jesus people" and going to Bible studies. I didn't think I needed to make any changes in my life, and besides, I thought it was just a phase she was going through; it wouldn't last. And my life was much too exciting to bother with the question of God. Pam and I headed in opposite directions.

On a positive side note, Pam had not stopped praying for me, had not stopped wondering whether I'd given my life to the Lord.

At one point, not too long ago, she searched around for me on the Internet, hoping to reunite and possibly share the Good News with me again. She didn't find me, but Bethany's name kept coming up in the searches. She'd heard of Bethany Hamilton, yet she had no idea that I was Bethany's mother until she picked up a copy of Bethany's book. You can imagine her joy and surprise! She'd found me; and wonder of wonders! I was a believer and had a family that was totally passionate about God.

In September 2008, she wrote me a letter. Not long after that, I called her. We've kept in touch since then. What a beautiful thing is friendship made complete with fellowship and prayer. It has been such a blessing to realize that every spiritual seed that someone plants is God's responsibility; and though Pamela was unaware that the seeds she had planted when we were teenagers were taking root in my life, God knew.

But back then, I was still as far from God as I knew how to be. I was going to college and I was surfing as much as I could. I was even entering contests. One contest, held in Baja, California, put me in the ranks of the best women surfers of the era. Too bad my beautiful prized board was stolen from where we were staying.

My boyfriend and I rented a cute house just above a notorious part of San Diego, called Ocean Beach. OB, as the locals call it, was the surfer and hippie haven of San Diego. Drugs were everywhere, and parties raged all night. In spite of all this, or in denial of it, our plan was to get through college and get married when we were both 21.

I took the first job available, at a nearby Kentucky Fried Chicken, while Tony made surfboards in the garage. When I'd come home at night, our house was filled with stoned and starving surfers. I was a welcome sight, since I would always bring home leftover chicken or cream pies.

There was a notice put up at our college offering a course on Transcendental Meditation, by Maharishi Mahesh Yogi, the guy the Beatles followed. I was interested, because it was supposed to help your mental faculties work better, or so the advertisement said. I had a hunger for knowledge, and I thought this would help my memory. Then I found that it cost $30—quite a sum at that time. It made me mad. I thought that it seemed religious in a way and should be free. (I learned later from my husband, Tom, that he took this course at the same time I was considering it, and he even got his special Hindu "god" name to chant—all for just 30 bucks!) So it was just a religious exercise to earn some brownie points, not the learning tool I thought it was supposed to be.

Work and school were like blips on my radar screen compared to surfing. Southern California is ripe with incredible surf spots, so I was able to bloom where I was planted. While localism was widespread in those days and is still very much alive and well at just about every break in the world, as a girl, I had to battle and strategize and earn every wave I caught. Parties have never interested me, so I didn't have a problem with going to bed early. That meant that I could get up before light and be at the beach for an early morning sunrise session before the waves got too crowded. The early morning dawn patrol became my routine for the next 30 years.

I had invited my boyfriend to go skiing for his birthday, so we jumped into my little red Volkswagen Karmann Ghia and went up to ski the slopes of Big Bear, California. Before surfing dominated my life, I'd gone skiing with my family pretty often, so I knew what I was doing. My boyfriend, however, had never skied before. But he was cocky. I guess he figured his surfing prowess would serve him well on the slopes.

It didn't. I finally went off to ski by myself . . . to leave some part of his ego intact. To his credit, by noon he'd advanced far enough to venture onto the intermediate runs; and by the time we were heading home, he was even enthused about this new sport. Maybe too enthused.

A month or so later, some friends of his suggested a ski trip to Mammoth, the central California snow paradise. I had a new job working at a health food restaurant called the Homestead, so I couldn't go.

A week passed, and Tony never came back. But a letter did. He'd gotten a job working the lifts and had a new life now as a "ski bum," a new life that didn't include me. I was left alone with an empty house and a few surfboards.

I was heartbroken. I'm sure that all the customers at work couldn't help but notice my dejected demeanor, especially that young guy fresh off his tour of duty who had moved out to Ocean Beach to surf between classes at Mesa College. His name was Tom Hamilton. And, yes, he did attend Mesa College at the same time that I took classes there; and he may even have dropped in on my waves at Sunset Cliffs, or maybe I dropped in on his!

Hawaii Bound

*If I rise on the wings of the dawn, if I settle on the
far side of the sea, even there your hand will guide me,
your right hand will hold me fast.*

PSALM 139:9-10, *NIV*

I spent a night in jail for eating evidence. Allegedly, it was a very, very small pot plant. Not a leaf, but a seedling. Oddly enough, it wasn't even mine, nor was I actually in trouble over it; it was just the final straw in a series of misadventures. But if I hadn't been thrown in jail; if I hadn't destroyed that miniscule piece of evidence that wasn't even against me; and if I hadn't been mad and maybe just a little crazy, I might never have decided to leave California for Hawaii.

Going back in time to Ocean Beach, my boyfriend had abandoned me and moved to Mammoth with his friends. Brokenhearted, I struggled to pay the rent as I worked at the Homestead health food restaurant, the very same restaurant my future husband frequented. But it would be far too simple a story for me to have noticed him then. I was too focused on everyday life, either at work or in the water, even though he often surfed the same spots I did.

It was a very lonely time for me. I felt as if I were not tethered to anything. And because I was young and maybe a bit naïve, I imagined that if I went up to Mammoth, I could patch things up with my ex-boyfriend—even though he had told me in his letter that we were over.

I moved out of my cottage and drove my little Karman Ghia up to Mammoth Mountain. Tony's friends had put a wall between us, so I ended up renting a room in a house from a guy who was managing it for the owners. I soon found a job punching lift tickets. You could say that things were a bit strained. There were plenty of people my age, many of them surfers when not on the slopes; and while I was busy with work, I still managed to get in my fair share of skiing. In the end, the challenge of becoming a good skier overrode the relationship woes that had brought me to the mountain.

There was a couple that rented the room next to me. I hardly ever saw them, and I never talked to them; but I'd hear them arguing at night or just making a racket. Their schedule was unpredictable; they came and went at weird hours, sometimes disappearing for days on end. Unlike the typical friendly folks in this small mountain town, they were extremely private.

One day, I ran into my fellow boarder as he rushed out of his door to use the bathroom. He nodded quickly at me, never saying a word. His hand was wrapped in a rough bandage with blood seeping through.

Later that afternoon, as I was coming home from work, police had surrounded the house. They had his girlfriend, but she wasn't in custody, because he was the one they wanted. It turns out that he was a bank robber and had been shot through the hand during his last hold-up. They had finally tracked him back here, the house where I lived, through the license plates on his stolen RV!

The sheriff interrogated me. "Did you know him? What was he doing here?" I explained that my housemates had been a total mystery to me. This situation now made a whole lot more sense to me.

The next day, I was asked to come down to the police station, and I assumed it was to make a statement about my former housemate, the bank robber. But I was whisked into an interrogation room and grilled about the alleged pot plants the police had found on the landlord's porch.

"What pot plants?" I asked, because I truly had no idea that the landlord was growing pot. That's when they brought out these two plants no bigger than my thumbnail.

The officers started to increase the pressure. They wanted me to tell them that my landlord was part of a drug ring and that he was growing marijuana. I'd never seen any sign that he was dealing drugs, and I wasn't about to get him in trouble for something that I had no knowledge of.

After turning the screws without results, one of the officers said (just like in a bad police drama), "We'll give you some time to think this over," and then walked out of the interrogation room, leaving me alone with the tiny plants. I was annoyed and angry about getting hassled—angry that they wanted me to blame my landlord just so they could get a bigger bust. Angry that they'd dragged me down here for these two little alleged pot plants.

I guess I was so incensed that I decided the easiest thing to do was eat the evidence. Which is exactly what I did! You should have seen the looks on their faces when they returned.

Needless to say, they were unhappy with me. It earned me a night in jail.

Looking back, I bet I would have been more cooperative in the first place if they'd just told me that my landlord had skipped town with all the rent he'd been collecting for several months. The real bummer was that the jail they took me to was in Bishop, California, which was an hour's drive away. When they booted me onto the street the following day, I had no way to get back to my car parked at the police station in Mammoth. I thought about hitchhiking, but instead started calling a few friends I knew back in Mammoth to ask for a ride. I finally reached Chris, one of the surf crew, and one of the guys I knew through Tony, my ex-boyfriend.

Feeling free and having a need to de-stress, I left the police station and headed down the remote mountain road to meet up with Chris. I grew wary when a Chevy van, traveling in the opposite direction, slowed down and the driver asked me if I needed a ride. I said, "No, thanks," so he drove on; but then, looking behind me, I saw him make a U-turn back toward me. Alarm bells went off! At that moment, Chris, looking a bit like a hippie, came along to pick me up in his brown Volkswagen camper van. In retrospect, I could see God's hand of protection on my life.

As we drove back to Mammoth, Chris and I talked about Hawaii and how much fun it would be to surf there. Spring was coming, the snow was melting—and with it my job. I didn't have a place to live, thanks to bank robbers and an embezzling bonsai-pot grower for a landlord. It seemed to be the perfect time to make a radical change in plans. Chris asked me if he could tag along.

Instead of going to Oahu, where all the famous surf breaks are, Chris suggested that we go to the island of Kauai. I had never heard of it. He had friends who lived there and would put us up, and from what he'd heard, the waves were uncrowded.

I agreed. Kauai it was! We sold our cars, packed our surfboards and were off to the islands and my destiny, the place where I was meant to be.

All this time, Tom was settling into college classes in San Diego. The G.I. bill paid for his education and housing costs. He condensed his classes together into two days so he would have plenty of open time to surf.

When Tom was first discharged from the Navy, he'd gone home to New Jersey. But he quickly scraped up enough cash by hustling at local pool halls (and polishing his reputation as the "Trickster") to return to San Diego, where the surf was more to his liking.

Surfing was undergoing an emerging revolution during this time. Long, heavy surfboards had given way to shorter, lighter and more maneuverable ones. The day of "hanging ten" (hanging all 10 toes off the front of a long board) was fading out. On a short board a surfer plants his feet and uses his core body weight to turn and carve the open face of the wave, staying just ahead of the whitewater foam.

Then the surf leash came along. Previously, if a surfer wiped out, he or she would have to swim after his (her) surfboard, usually all the way to the beach. One would think this idea of a leash on the board would make all surfers shout hallelujah and save countless wasted time swimming after boards in cold water, or crab-crawling over sharp reefs. But a bunch of surfers who considered themselves hardcore looked down on anyone who paddled out with a leash, calling them kooks. In fact, the early leashes were called "kook cords." Even I refused to use a leash, as I was a very strong swimmer. But the kooks with leashes were getting a lot more waves, while hard-core guys were swimming after their boards. Eventually, almost every surfer went out and bought a leash.

Tom, like me, had been harboring the idea of going to Hawaii. He loved the surf in California, but he longed to find even more challenging waves—such as the ones he always saw in surf movies or magazines. The words of his Hawaiian shipmate, Rob, kept echoing in his ears. After only a year of school, on Christmas break, he took all of his savings and bought a round-trip ticket to Honolulu.

He knew enough to get out of town, as Honolulu was called, and head for the countryside of the island. He was on the prowl for the bigger, more powerful waves. And they could only be found on the North Shore, where the surf breaks had familiar names that Tom had read about in the surf magazines filled with pictures of powerful pounding waves: Pipeline, Sunset Beach, Waimea Bay.

Tom found a room to share with some other mainland transplants. Surfing the North Shore with them, Tom increased his skill level in bigger waves. Within two years, his roommates would become legendary big-wave surfers.

A friend suggested that Tom shouldn't leave the islands without checking out a more remote island in Hawaii. "Go visit Kauai," he said. "That's where you'll find a more relaxed, slow-paced life." And so it was his destiny, in response to a suggestion by a friend, and with just a few days left in his trip, that Tom landed at the Lihue airport on Kauai.

At the time, the runway wasn't big enough to handle jets, so you had to fly in on noisy, rattling prop-planes. The gate was a pavilion with a few benches and a chain-link fence. The luggage carousel was just a 20-foot-long steel-covered piece of plywood.

Tom couldn't help but contrast the Garden Isle to bustling Oahu. With his backpack and surfboards slung over his back, Tom hiked out onto the main street, a one-lane road that didn't even circle completely around the whole island. To this day the sheer cliffs of the Na Pali coast make a connecting road impracticable, so not a whole lot has changed since that time.

Tom didn't know anyone, nor did he know where anything was; he just knew one name: Hanalei Bay, where the waves were supposed to be the best. But he was a resourceful young man with a sleeping bag, a little cash and a surfboard. It would be an adventure. So naturally he stuck his thumb out for a ride.

It wasn't long before an older Hawaiian guy in a pickup asked in thick Pidgin English, "Where you like go?"

"Hanalei," said Tom, mangling the pronunciation like so many tourists do.

The driver motioned to the back of the truck and Tom climbed in. To his amusement, he found that he was sharing the ride to Hanalei with a couple of caged pigs and a load of pig slop.

Amazingly, the guy (who happened to be Henry Tai Hook, the honorary mayor of Kauai's North Shore) dropped him off in the center of Hanalei town. Tom thanked him, grabbed his gear and headed to the beach. For the next couple of days, he camped out and surfed the north shore of Kauai, hiding his belongings in the bushes while surfing.

It took only those few days of breathtaking beauty, lush jungle, majestic waterfalls and crystal-blue waves to get Tom thoroughly hooked. He had his roommate in San Diego ship over the rest of his belongings. Then he enrolled in the small junior college and declared Kauai his new home.

The early seventies were the beginning of a dramatic demographic shift for the state of Hawaii. The chieftains had eventually made surfing strictly a royal sport; commoners were forbidden from surfing under penalty of death. The local islanders, heavily made up of a pan-Asian and Polynesian people, had outnumbered the *haoles,* as Caucasian people are called.

But the hundred-year-old agricultural economy that had made the island a melting pot by importing labor from Portugal, China, Korea, Japan and the Philippines was being superseded by a new boom to an old industry: tourism. Tourism not only brought visitors from the mainland, but also people who liked what they saw moved to the islands. For a while the outer islands were mostly immune, but during the time when Tom and I separately and unrelatedly moved to Kauai, there was a surge of mainland surfers coming to Hawaii.

Maybe it had something to do with surfing going beyond a simple craze of the early sixties; maybe it had to do with the political and sociological turbulence of the times. Whatever it was, those who considered themselves "local" (even though the undiluted indigenous Hawaiian population had shrunk to a tiny percentile) found themselves swamped by young strangers from the mainland showing up at surf spots dominated for years by locals.

Needless to say, sparks often flew.

Since the time when Captain James Cook first made contact in the late 1700s, Hawaii had become a melting pot of cultures as successive waves of immigrants came in; but by the second or third generation, they had become firmly rooted in closely interconnected relationships—people who had known each other since birth, the famous family, or *ohana*—where everyone was somehow related to everyone else. They even spoke a unique dialect: Pidgin English.

Throw a bunch of surfers and hippies into the mix, fresh from the craziest period of American cultural change, the sixties, and you had a recipe for conflict.

Tom was remarkably good at avoiding trouble. He understood that there was a pecking order in the surfing lineup, and that he would need to spend considerable time developing relationships with the locals in order to gain some kind of hesitant acceptance. It didn't matter how well he surfed, he had to make good with them on another level. Besides, Tom naturally has a laid-back, non-confrontational kind of personality.

That didn't always keep him out of trouble.

As he had done in New Jersey, Tom would unleash the "Trickster" at a pool hall whenever he needed to scrape together some extra cash. He wasn't a fool about it; he'd just win a couple of bucks here and there so no one would notice that the lucky young *haole* surfer was actually a pool hustler.

But one night, in Hanalei's infamous Tahiti Nui Bar, Tom was naively cleaning out some of the local heavyweights using his skills with the cue ball. As these guys simmered they got quieter, so Tom didn't see their anger escalating as they continued drinking. Suddenly, out of nowhere, one of them swung a cue stick at Tom's head. His quick reflexes saved him as he brought up his own stick in the nick of time. It shattered from the blow, but better that than his skull. Tom wisely decided to give the "Trickster" a rest for a while and got a job harvesting taro.

On occasion, Tom's red Kharmin Ghia (another uncanny coincidence?) broke down when he commuted to and from Kauai Community College. There weren't many people with cars heading north at that time of the night, and even fewer were willing to stop for a longhaired hippie. Sometimes Tom would get stranded part of the way back with no prospect of getting home, and then the rain would kick in. Kauai is the wettest spot on earth, after all.

Resourceful, as well as gutsy, Tom figured out that many of the churches along the way were seldom locked. He spent a number of nights stretched out on a pew with the minister's robe draped over him to stay warm. Of course, Tom was always gone before dawn, having carefully hung up his makeshift blanket where he had found it, all ready for the next Sunday morning.

It was as close to a church service as Tom had been for years. After finishing junior college on the GI bill, Tom headed to Oahu in order to continue his education at the University of Hawaii. While living at Rocky Point on the North Shore, he became a polished surfer. With his genial ways, he became friends with many of the iconic figures of surfing at that time: Steve Cranston, Tom Parish, Jackie Dunn and Greg Lohr. Tom shadowed Jerry Lopez to determine his takeoff from the lineup at Pipeline. He often surfed Sunset when Barry Kanaiaupuni and Eddie Aikau were out. These legendary Hawaiian surfers represented the heart and soul of the surfing community.

Back in the '70s, compared to Kauai, Oahu was a rat race. The surf spots were crowded and dog-eat-dog. Racial tensions were escalating, and episodes of intimidation were getting more frequent, culminating in the brutal beating of a group of famous Australian and South African surfers. There were even death threats serious enough to require police escorts to and from surf contests.

On top of these conflicts, there were the drugs and drug dealers, and the slow unraveling of the "Summer of Love" into a fractured, territorial hostility. Yet, among the hedonist and hippie surfers, something powerful was taking place.

Big-wave surfer Rick Irons was busy in his shaping room when Tom came in to have a custom surfboard made. Rick, uncle of the late world champion surfer Andy Irons and his accomplished brother Bruce, was a fascinating character who had been a U.S. champion in the sixties.

"Say, Rick," Tom said, "what's up with all the little fish you draw on the boards you shape?" Rick smiled and told him the fish was a sign that he was a follower of Jesus Christ. He then proceeded to share Christ and the forgiveness that was his because Christ died for his sins on the cross. Tom recalls that this was the first time anyone had ever shared the good news of salvation through Jesus Christ with him.

It wasn't just Rick Irons sharing this "good news." Other young surfers around Tom were discovering a powerful relationship with God as well. North Shore surfers Mike Stangel and Bill Stonebraker also became Christians and, along with Rick, went on to become pastors.

Tom remembers hearing worship songs pouring out of the second story windows of Billy Barnfields's place, another popular surfboard shaper. "I was curious and knew it was some kind of Bible study, but nobody had invited me, and I was too shy to ask," Tom says, on reflection.

Up and down the seven-mile stretch of North Shore beaches, God was working in the lives of young, healthy and talented men and women within the surfing community. Some of them, like Tom, were hearing the good news of Jesus Christ for the first time—and not from some glossy evangelist or at a stuffy church service, but from someone they knew and respected—surfers and shapers. The relationship was the most effective way for the message to be spread—organically, and friend to friend, in this ocean-minded community.

While living at Rocky Point, Tom got to surf some of the most beautiful breaks on the North Shore. One day, he got a call from a friend back on Kauai telling him about a job as a banquet waiter at a resort there. The pay was great and the evening hours were perfect for a surfer. It was all the encouragement Tom needed to leave Oahu behind and catch a puddle jumper back to Kauai.

I know that a 21-year-old girl heading off to Hawaii with some guy she barely knows was not the average thing to do. But I left for Hawaii with Chris, a surfing friend and traveling partner, who liked to do the same things I did.

It was also a very strange era, with folk rocker Stephen Stills singing, "Love the One You're With." We would end up being roommates with . . . privileges.

Once we were on Kauai, we stayed a couple of weeks with the friends that Chris knew well and grew up with. They let us stay in their attic. It was hot, dusty and full of spider webs. The only furnishing was a queen-sized mattress, but we were stoked because our only goal was to surf and hang out on the beach as much as we could.

It was a surprise to us when the hostess said, "Well, two weeks is long enough to have visitors. Aloha!" Being young and self-absorbed, I guess we thought we could live in their home and eat their food indefinitely, especially because she was such a great cook.

We decided to pool our money and eventually buy a van that we could live in, figuring that it would be a cheap and leak-proof way to surf all over the island. So we went out and camped on the beach until we were able to find a van. It didn't take long to come up with the $500.

It was summertime, when the surf is normally flat on the North Shore; but there were lots of other things to do: diving, fishing or hiking the Hanakapi'ai trail along the face of the sheer Napali Cliffs to a magnificent valley and huge waterfall.

What we mostly did was pick up puka shells. These are small disk-shaped shells, actually the remains of a larger shell, with a hole (*puka*, in Hawaiian) in the center. They were strung together to make a puka shell necklace, which were, in the early seventies, all the rage. Islanders who had been walking over these shells all their lives suddenly realized that a can full of these fairly common little shells could net over $50—a significant sum at that time.

Our van was parked across from the huge cave and right in front of a surf spot appropriately enough called Tunnels. Living in our van near Haena Beach Park, we saw that some families had roped off entire areas of the beach to keep others from mining their "claim," not unlike the gold rush in early California.

Chris and I decided that it would be simpler to find our puka shells underwater, so we spent much of the summer snorkeling around the shallows with an empty soda can in our hands, turning up the sand for the little shells. This activity kept us in shape and ready to surf when the waves returned.

Tunnels reef was the first place I ever surfed in Kauai. It was about the only place on the north side of the island that had waves during the summer. I never liked the wave all that much, because it dumped on a shallow reef, and I always came back in with cuts all over my feet. The wave runs along a deep drop-off channel, which was very spooky and a haven for sharks.

I couldn't know then that this surf break would feature so largely in my life story; for it was at Tunnels that a shark attacked my daughter, Bethany, many years later.

Captured by Christ

You did not choose Me but I chose you, and appointed you that you would go and bear fruit, and that your fruit would remain, so that whatever you ask of the Father in My name He may give to you.

JOHN 15:16, *NASB*

I keep telling people who hear about our past that Tom and I were *not* hippies.

The distinction to most people isn't that great; but in my mind, even back then, it was important. What consumed me was the addiction of surfing, not dropping out, not political activism or communing with anything other than a nice glassy wave at an uncrowded beach or reef break.

Every waking moment I spent strategizing my daily plan to find and catch the best waves. I was the epitome of a *Soul Surfer*.

Hippies . . . well, hippies were the people living in Taylor Camp.

In the late 1960s, Howard Taylor, brother of actress Elizabeth Taylor, bought a chunk of land way out near the end of the road on Kauai. He wanted to build a house, but the state wouldn't grant him a permit to develop it; instead they wanted to condemn the empty land and then add it to nearby Ke'e Lagoon at the end of the road.

Taylor got fed up with the grasping state when they told him to pay taxes on the land they were trying to condemn; so in 1969, Taylor invited a bunch of hippies to camp out on his property free of charge.

Located near Tunnels Beach, Taylor Camp became a magnet for peaceniks who built lean-tos and bamboo tree houses out of found materials. They formed a primitive communal society, with few rules and even fewer clothing requirements, at the extreme edge of paradise.

Elizabeth Tayor's son joined Taylor Camp. On a visit to Kauai, her son presented her with a puka shell necklace. This touched off the puka necklace craze when she was photographed later while wearing the gift.

Taylor Camp was razed by the state in 1977, but it still looms large in the North Shore legends.

I spent my days scouring the North Shore looking for surf. Kauai's natural beauty captivates you at every turn. From the end of the road on the north side, to the end of the road on the west coast, God's creation rings loud and clear. We parked wherever we could, usually near surf breaks or free showers. But after a summer of close quarters, I decided to go back to California. As far as I was concerned, Chris was only a friend, and I was feeling claustrophobic.

I thank God every day for His divine hand during this point of my journey, even though I was far from Him. There were few things constant in my life except for surfing, and it would serve no good purpose to itemize the foolish choices I made. Suffice it to say, I spent the next few years bouncing around from Kauai to California to Oahu to Maui and then back to Kauai, usually showing up with a bit of cash, a few belongings and an agenda for surfing adventures.

Along the way, I collected my fair share of heartbreak, wounds, regrets and guilt. These emotions I stuffed down into the recesses of my soul. But they wouldn't heal, and later bubbled up and burned like acid. The proverbial hole in my heart kept getting bigger. While a lot of my friends dealt with their purposelessness by diving headlong into alcohol or drugs, I found that surfing took away the emptiness for a while.

In a way, surfing became my drug of choice. I lived for the rush of adrenaline when I flew across the waves. I lived for the challenge of ever-bigger surf. And I forgot my troubles in my exhaustion at the end of the day in a paradise filled with rainbows.

By the time I ended up back on Kauai, I was once again living in the back of a station wagon—not with Chris, but with another guy, in a very similar kind of relationship.

While all this was going on with me, Tom was getting to be a well-known surfer in Kauai's North Shore lineup. But unlike me, he was flying solo. In fact, with all the young male surfers migrating to Hawaii, the guy/girl ratio of our age group (under 35) was so skewed that many lonely guys referred to Kauai as "Monk Island."

Tom had landed a great job as a banquet waiter at a large resort called the Kauai Surf, a hotel that still stands, now a Marriot. The only problem was that he was living on the North Shore, and the hotel was all the way into town, quite a distance, particularly with a car like Tom's VW van that wasn't always working.

I first noticed Tom as he pulled up into the dirt parking lot at Pine Trees. Actually, I noticed his car first, a clean-looking VW camper van. My interest in cars came from my dad's after-hours job at a dealership when he would come home from work with a new car almost every night.

The car made me take a second look at the handsome surfer boy.

Tom knew my "boyfriend," and we all went surfing together that day. The first thing I noticed was that Tom was goofy footed (right foot forward on the board). All the guys that I had ever had a crush on were goofy footers, so I thought to myself, *Uh oh, what might this mean?*

I also took notice that he could surf quite well, especially in big waves.

My living conditions had finally upgraded to a house instead of a station wagon, and I could actually cook an honest-to-goodness meal. As a result, we started inviting Tom over for breakfast from time to time after a morning surf session. (He still says I can cook up a "mean breakfast.")

I was strongly attracted to him from day one, but Tom assumed that I was romantically linked to my friend.

It was complicated.

By this time, I was ready to get out of the relationship. Maybe part of me knew that I was just drifting and going through the motions. I had been threatening to break off the relationship for quite a while, but my companion always seemed to finagle me to stay a little longer.

Though we now lived in a house, I had to get out on my own. I moved out and rented a room. I got a job. It was exhilarating! Then Tom asked me out.

I was expectant and hopeful; I was flattered and excited. My interest in him had grown over the months as our acquaintance deepened. When he found out I'd called it quits with the other guy, he was ready to step in.

It was a whirlwind romance . . . or maybe it was just the cup of psychedelic mushrooms we shared that first night, but we moved in together after our first date. Unlike anything else I'd known before, it was pretty obvious that this relationship was going to be a serious one.

Something odd happened within me, which I can't quite explain: I decided that I wanted to be in a proper relationship with Tom when he proposed to me. Something inside me was yearning to find propriety, so I told Tom that I wanted to rent my own place. I moved into a house with a surfer friend name Loli.

I got more than I bargained for.

Loli was a brand-new, on-fire Christian, and she was excited about her newfound faith. She was up every morning at 5:00 A.M., reading her Bible; I only know this because I was up at 5:00 A.M. every morning heading out to find surf. She invited me to church, but I always brushed her off. I couldn't, however, stop her words and her example from watering the spiritual seeds planted in my heart at Emmanuel Vacation Bible School so long ago.

Tom proposed to me on my birthday, which was Valentine's Day. I burst into tears right there in the restaurant. We married on August 25, 1979, with a very fun, laid-back, island-style wedding, complete with ukuleles, volleyball, homemade *lilikoi* juice, a homemade wedding dress and an Aloha shirt I made from white satin for Tom. Our banquet feast was potluck with imu-style (baked in an underground oven) turkey.

The day was perfect and beautiful and 100 percent ours. But if a swell had come in, we probably would have postponed the whole thing to go surfing!

We were married in a ceremony right on the beach in Hanalei, by a chain-smoking Catholic priest. For the longest time, Tom's mom insisted that we were not really married because the vows were not spoken in a sanctified church building. (We assured her that the priest told us that beach weddings were okay in Hawaii.) I remember that Loli read from 1 Corinthians 13, the Bible's love chapter. I'd never heard it before, and I was surprised that words so beautiful were in the Bible.

Many people head to Hawaii for their honeymoon, but we went to New Jersey. We stayed with Tom's folks in the house where Tom grew up, which was not my dream honeymoon suite.

When we returned to Kauai, we spent six weeks in Moloaa in a beautiful house near the beach, house-sitting for friends. This became the real honeymoon, but it almost became a very short marriage. While lighting the gas pilot, Tom was blown across the kitchen with his hair in flames!

When the honeymoon was over, we moved into our new home: a VW van.

It's okay to roll your eyes (I can't see you). I wanted to be your typical new bride who can hardly wait to color coordinate her new nest and try out recipes on her husband. But the truth was that I really wanted to surf.

We both worked at the same hotel, and we were on the same schedule. We were saving money by living in the van; and when we had days off, we would cruise the North Shore looking for uncrowded waves. The problem was that our *hale* on wheels—our van—kept breaking down. Every time the mechanic, Ross, would fix it, something else would go wrong. It was as if the thing was cursed!

Looking back on it now, I think that maybe the van was actually blessed. I don't know if God would actually go so far as to mess with the mechanics of a Volkswagen van, but I think He did! What felt like a real pain for Tom and me led us to Christ.

Three unlikely characters, all surfers, were instrumental in drawing both Tom and me to the place where God wanted us. The three of them shared a house in Wailua on the east side of Kauai.

One of the guys, nicknamed "Creature" because of his car, "The Creature Mobile" (an old clunker he'd covered with plastic figurines held on by super-glue), had the wild distinction of being tossed in the loony bin for one drug-addled adventure. In his confused mind, he became so convinced that he was John the Baptist that he marched into a church service and took over the microphone, trying to get disciples. (He jokes around that he got no disciples at the church service, but he made lots of them in the mental ward.)

Creature had first migrated to Santa Cruz, California, where he quickly became a fixture in the local surf community. At that time, he had become friends with Michel Junod, one of the three roommates, and a highly respected (to this day) surfboard shaper and surfer, and on occasion, successful competitor. The two of them eventually drifted to Oahu's North Shore where they spent several seasons riding the massive tubes of the Banzai Pipeline and other daredevil big-wave spots before moving into a place together on Kauai.

The third roommate was Mark Nakatsukasa, a reed-thin wanderer who had traveled in his VW bus through Mexico and Central America, questing for perfect, undiscovered waves.

This adventure refined his car repair skills. Whenever our van broke down (all of the time), we would sit around on the lawn exchanging surf stories with Mark as he worked on our bus. We all shared the same free-spirited view of life. What Tom and I didn't know was that Mark was going through a turbulent internal revolution.

The carefree Mark we thought we knew was a façade. He was secretly wrestling with a deep emptiness he'd tried to fill with waves, adventure and drugs. Nothing kept away the oppressive despair that weighed down on him day after day; and not one of us knew that he was quietly contemplating suicide.

Mark had encountered some committed Christian men who had, for some annoying reason, decided to make Mark, Creature and Michel the subject of their prayers. This group of guys referred to the three surfing roommates as "Mission Impossible": *impossible for man, but possible for God.*

Mark got riled up about being witnessed to, so one day he picked up a Bible in order to find ammo within its pages to disprove its message. As with many others who have begun this way, the end result was quite different from the original goal. It wasn't long before Michel and Creature's faith also erupted, and the three new believers in our world turned everything upside down.

Ross, the one who usually helped us fix our van, was at his wit's end and turned us and our broken van over to Mark. Eventually, Mark invited us to park our van in his driveway so he could repair it, since we had no work for two weeks and practically lived there anyway.

We'd been living in the van for four months, and it was nice to have a real house to retreat to. The three guys had a lot of tracts and comics with a Christian message lying around. At first I was put off, but eventually I picked up a booklet. I was fascinated that Jesus had fulfilled over 300 prophecies about

His life and His purpose to bring us into a right relationship with His Father.

Creature, Michel and Mark were all fired up about their new relationship with Jesus. I don't remember feeling offended at all. Creature laughingly says that he "hammered" on us for weeks in his hyper-excitable manner that many today would back away from. The guys' enthusiasm caught my attention. Their passion was like listening to guys who had the ultimate surf stoke. Tom thought they were crazy—"bonzai" for Jesus.

Something deep within me was responding to what they were talking about. I was awakening to truth I couldn't turn away from.

When Tom and I first started hanging around Mark's house, the guys were constantly playing a Frank Zappa album that had notorious lyrics. Apparently, they didn't see the conflict between what was blaring out of their speakers and the new life they were proclaiming . . . but I did. And I said something about it.

"If you guys are supposed to be Christians, why do you listen to this?" I was genuinely asking because I thought it mattered. I guess it made sense to them, too, because the next thing I knew there was a whole new collection of albums being played. (Mark went so far as to break the offending records so he wouldn't be tempted to play them.) Most of the music they replaced was by young Christian artists. Keith Green replaced Frank Zappa.

To have music that revolved around God and His Word deepened my passion for music, which was already strong and has been passed on to my own kids today. This experience brought me to the most important decision of my life. I prayed to God for a personal relationship with Jesus Christ. I now believed that He had paid for my sins when He died on the cross and rose from the dead; that He had conquered death and He would return for me someday to live with Him forever.

I remember to this day where I was when I gave my life to Christ. I was standing next to our white VW van in Mark's driveway. It was the beginning of a relationship with the God who had been courting me my entire life.

Tom and I began to go to home Bible studies in Kalaheo. The first was at the home of a local surf shop owner, Tim Huggins, whose shop also served as a small Christian bookstore. These Bible studies were aimed at people like us and were a far cry from the typical church.

At this point in my spiritual life I still had a lot of growing to do. The only thing I knew was "Jesus loves me, this I know." As far as the Bible was concerned, there was no reason that I would read that book. It probably came from my environment growing up, but at the time, the Bible seemed to me to be the last book on earth I wanted to read.

It took six months of being a Christian before I realized that I needed to get to know God better by reading His Word. So I went to the Christian bookstore Lihue Surf and Bible and bought a Bible for myself.

Tom, because of the devoutness of his parents, and his time in parochial school, had a familiarity with the Bible and a concept of salvation through Christ. He even considered himself a "Christian." But it was the day when he stood in the surfboard shaping room with Rick Irons, asking about why Rick drew those little fishes, that Tom understood that living Christianity is a *relationship* with Christ and not intellectually subscribing to a set of beliefs. It wasn't just knowledge; it was a relationship.

Yes, he stood by me and affirmed my decision to say yes to Christ, but it wasn't until after we'd been going to Bible studies that he reached his choice to walk away from selfishness and toward God's unconditional love.

At the end of one meeting, something the speaker said hit Tom hard. (Tom says, "God busted me.") All of a sudden, he broke down, the emotional response of surrendering his life to Christ. He knew that now, after sitting at the doorstep for so long, he truly was starting a new life in Christ.

Tom followed up his decision by getting baptized in the hot tub after Bible study. Even though almost all churches in Hawaii use the warm tropical Pacific, Tom felt that he wanted to show his faith immediately by being baptized that very same night.

As Tom and I awakened to our new life, we realized with joy that the network of Christian surfers was much deeper and more widespread than we had ever known. It turned out that there were a lot of other young people who were just like us and had become believers; they were people looking for love, purpose and vision in their lives. Few of us had family nearby, but in Jesus we now had a family of brothers and sisters to share our lives with.

It was also a struggle at times to get my independent mind into an understanding of the Christian life. I remember the first time I ever attended a Sunday morning service after getting saved. The pastor teaching it said that Christians shouldn't smoke pot. *I didn't want to be told what to do!*

In essence, I still wanted to be in charge of my life. It was fine to invite Jesus to come sit on the couch in my heart, but He'd better not start moving furniture around or poking into those dark corners. It took a while for the Holy Spirit to transform my life. It was a struggle because I had spent so many years doing whatever I wanted without answering to anyone. I had to come to grips with the fact that not only was Jesus my Savior, but He was also my *Lord.*

Tom and I spent the early months of our marriage surfing the island in our VW van, going to Bible studies, hanging out with fellow surfers who, like us, had encountered Christ, and attending church every Sunday at Garden Island Christian Fellowship in Hanalei.

New swells were on the horizon. . . . Michel spent time as a missionary in South America before moving back to Santa Cruz, California, where he shapes beautiful custom boards. He is an icon in the surfboard-making industry, yet he gives all the glory to Christ.

Creature became a founding pastor of a church, Kauai Christian Fellowship, on the south side of the island, known for its cutting-edge youth ministry and music.

Mark Nakatsukasa spent a number of years with YWAM (Youth With A Mission) as head of the School of Biblical Studies before moving to Thailand, where he currently runs an orphanage founded after the 2005 tsunami in an area that is predominantly Muslim.

Little did Tom and I know that God had prepared a path for us that would eventually walk us through loss and heartbreak to properly position us to become another voice to the world, declaring His love and salvation.

Raising Christian Kids on Kauai

As for me and my house, we will serve the LORD.

JOSHUA 24:15, *NASB*

I was seven months pregnant when I finally had to face the fact that I'd have to quit surfing. I could no longer pull it off in spite of using a longer board and even stuffing my bathing suit with foam to keep from falling off my growing belly while paddling.

I had always said that I would never have kids. I thought they would only get in the way of my surfing.

Love changed my mind.

Early in my pregnancy, the county condemned our illegal 12-by-12-foot shack that we called home. We didn't want to go back to living in our van, not with a baby on the way, so we had to find another house quickly. As the days passed, I felt frustration that my husband wasn't taking care of his pregnant wife by knocking down every door, beating every bush and doing whatever he could to find us a new place to live.

God had been working on me, so I decided I'd try a different approach from meekly ragging on him—which hadn't really worked anyhow. Instead of bugging Tom to find us a house, I decided to bug God.

At this stage of my Christian walk, I was still learning to pray—I was growing in my prayer life and learning to really talk to God and ask for His help. I was actually learning to *let* Him take over situations instead of making things worse by worrying about them.

As Tom and I immersed ourselves in the Bible, and as we watched other couples our age start families, it became clear to me that children are a good gift direct from God, especially when I read Scripture like "Children are a gift from the LORD; they are a reward from him" (Ps. 127:3, *NLT*).

So I prayed and asked God to help find us a new home.

No sooner had I finished asking God to help us than my husband came bursting through the door with great news. There was a place to rent in Hanalei, right near the beach, and within a short walk to one of our favorite surf spots. It even had indoor toilets! I looked upward and gave thanks, marveling at such a quick answer to my prayer.

"I called the landlord, and it's ours!" Tom said.

Prayer works—our family has witnessed it. God hears the cries of our heart and works so that His mighty hand is revealed—which makes us praise Him even more.

I am reminded of the time when Tom fell off of a roof. The hotel where Tom worked was undergoing another makeover, and Tom's friend got him work as a roofer. They were replacing old wooden shakes on a two-story house when Tom slipped and slid over the edge. He had the presence of mind to push away from the edge to avoid spearing himself on what was below, but he still landed hard on the hedge.

The hospital determined that he had a broken pelvis and decided to Medevac him to Oahu, a 100-mile flight that is usually choppy and rough at the best of times. Our church immediately went to prayer, along with many of our friends at other churches around the island.

In mid flight, Tom said he felt the pain replaced by a warm sensation. When he arrived at the Oahu hospital, a puzzled doctor who was examining new X-rays of his pelvis told him that somehow the bones had reset themselves. Tom points to the fervent prayers that had been offered up for him.

Two years into our marriage, Tom and I welcomed our little baby, Noah, into the world. I think what surprised me about having a child was the incredible, immense love I felt for this captivating little person on first sight. I didn't expect it, but this explosive love appeared in full force the moment Noah was put in my arms.

When Noah was about three years old, the hotel where both Tom and I worked closed down for a few months for refurbishment. It was tight money-wise, but we made it work. However, when our hotel finally reopened, four out of eight of the banquet waitresses were pregnant. I was one of them. Apparently, we had too much time on our hands during furlough.

The only dip in the road to my second pregnancy was that because we weren't working during the hotel refurbishment, we had no health insurance when Timmy was born. To save the hospital expense, we decided to try a home birth with a midwife and doctor standing by. After a quick labor, our second son, Timmy, was born; but because he was suffering from jaundice, we ended up in the hospital anyway.

I remembered thinking that maybe I should only have one child because I could never have enough love for two. Then, when my second son, Timmy, arrived, I found that God had enlarged my heart with the capacity to love them both with equal intensity. (Although I do have to admit that being enraptured with our newborn, Timmy, we accidentally left Noah at Sunday School. When we got home, Tom said, "Where's Noah?" Embarrassed, we raced back to church. As for Noah, he was busy playing and never even missed us.)

Adjusting to this new chapter of our lives was challenging.

After a few months of being home with our baby, I had to go back to work. Because Tom and I both worked as banquet waiters in the same hotel, we were able to organize our schedules so that one of us worked mornings and the other worked evenings. We didn't see much of each other as we passed Noah and Timmy off to each other like little footballs; but by juggling our schedule, we were at least able to raise them without too many baby-sitters.

Every day with the boys, living so close to the beach, I watched the perfect waves breaking; and as I watched my friends paddling out into the surf, I admit that it was difficult for me. What I didn't quite realize at the time was that God uses children to help us "die to ourselves." I learned this in small increments, through small sacrifices and daily exercises of patience. Love motivated me to lay down my life, my personal interests for the sake of my little boys.

All new parents probably experience a shock at the way a new baby changes the old rhythm of life. In my case, understanding that I needed to put myself second or third or even last allowed me to encourage Tom to go out and get a bit of surf whenever he had a break. On occasion, when time allowed, I still went out surfing.

Now that we had a real house—and not just a shanty—I was rudely awakened to the fact that living in vans and cars had not prepared me to be much of a skilled housewife, especially when caring for a newborn baby for the first time. So I developed some quirky house-cleaning strategies that I still use today and have taught my youngsters to use as well. One can only be dubbed the infamous Laundry Basket Pick-Up.

When the house was cluttered with stuff everywhere—the sink overflowing with dishes, and clothes and baby things on the couch and floor—and someone stopped by for a visit, I'd yell out, "Just a minute!" hand the baby to Tom and grab a laundry basket. Then I'd race around the house, cramming stuff into the basket, no matter what it was, and take the overflowing basket of clutter evidence to the bathroom, stowing it behind the shower curtain. Then I'd run back and open the door to reveal a nice, well-kept living room for our guest.

Now, I can be an excellent housekeeper, but if you were to ever visit our house, you might not believe me. It seems that we're always running out the door to chase waves, get to church, get to school or work, or head off on some wild new adventure. There's little time to keep up with everyone's messes, including my own!

As one kid went to two, and then three, I got so overwhelmed with trying to keep up with the clutter that I would try coming up with ways to enlist everyone's help. When the kids were little, I came up with a way to at least get them to pick up some stuff, almost like a game. I'd tell them it was time for everyone to do a "10 pick up and put away," and then we'd run around making a dent in the clutter. As the kids got older, I increased the number of items to "100 pick up"! Of course, when I'd announce it was time for the "100 Pick Up" game, they would wince, but we all could see the results of working together on an · overwhelming situation.

To be frank, we live in a jumbled house, more often than not. Every person has to prioritize the important things in life, and for me, organizing everything and having a place for everything isn't that super high on my list. Plus, whenever I get busy, it gets even more difficult to keep things straight.

That's why this year I gave Tom one of his gifts a month and a half after Christmas. It wasn't the first time I'd forgotten where I hid a Christmas present only to find it once I got around to straightening out this or that closet. It has become a family joke: The busier Mom gets, the more it can be Christmas all year round!

So much for saving money.

With two kids, we decided to move into a larger house on the riverfront in Hanalei. One vivid memory is of Tom teaching Noah how to fish for tilapia in the river. Those were great times. Our home was tiny. It was the old single-wall construction, no drywall, just painted wood. It had a rusty tin roof that made the noise of a thousand tiny drummers when it rained. We loved it there.

What we lacked in monetary wealth we had in natural beauty and a simple lifestyle that many people long for. Here's a snapshot of our country life, Hawaiian style: Fruit "dripped" from trees; fish filled the rivers and ocean; pristine waves peeled along the point. Stepping out of our home, we could see the emerald-colored cliffs rising up into the clouds as waterfalls cascaded into the valley below. That was only one of the views; on the other side was the river as it met the turquoise ocean, surfers gracefully moving along the waves.

Because Tom and I were such water people, we made sure that our kids learned to be water babies. After all, when you live on an island, it's a good idea to acclimate your kids to it as soon as possible. We lived in a house on the beach for two years when Noah was one to three years old. I was very concerned that his independent mind might decide to enjoy the water when I wasn't looking. So I decided to give him a big-wave education to teach him to respect the ocean. I took him by the hand, and we stood in the shore break with the waves crashing against us. He could handle it because I was holding on to him. He never, ever went down to the water without Mom or Dad!

Noah was four years older than Timmy, and it wasn't long before we started to get him up and standing on a surfboard in the shallow water near the pier. I was definitely a pleased mom!

Each of our kids learned to swim early. Tom and I would take them often to a friend's pool or to the ocean. If a child has been around the water enough to the point where he enjoys it and is not fearful because of lack of familiarity, it is simple to teach him the basics of swimming. We took all of our kids to the local swim program as soon as they turned three.

Still, a parent should never stop being vigilant, because that fatherly awareness helped save Timmy's life when he was around three-and-a-half years old. Tom and I had taken the boys to surf the ankle-slapper waves in the shallows next to the Hanalei pier. I went surfing while Tom sat in the car as Bethany slept in her car seat. The boys were sharing a surfboard while Tom, parked near the pier, watched them over a surf magazine.

After sharing the surfboard with his little brother for the better part of an hour, Noah decided that he wanted it all for himself, and he sent his little brother back to the beach. The water was shallow enough for Timmy to walk in, but a riptide had formed a few yards from the shore, racing parallel to the beach and creating a deep channel. Timmy, up to his chest in the shallow water, stepped right into it and was swept away.

Tom looked up just in time to see his youngest son hurtling toward the pier, tiny hand extended upward in a universal sign for help. Timmy, a quiet, peaceful child, never cried out as he was swept along; he just kept his head above water. Tom was already out of the car and running out onto the pier as he watched Timmy slip between the pilings and shoot out the other side toward the wide bay. Tom took off running, dived off the pier fully clothed and managed to grab Timmy just as he disappeared under water.

The church we were a part of began to grow as new people became believers and we all grew into spiritually healthy families together. God's Word became the backbone of our lives as we were blessed with many gifted Bible teachers visiting the islands. We loved celebrating Jesus together. Going to church was never a duty; it was a passion and a natural part of our lives. When the Word of God speaks to your heart, it becomes real and personal and helps you grow close to Him and trust Him with your life.

Since all of our kids are adults now, and in particular, since Bethany's story has gotten so much publicity, it is not uncommon for people to ask us our secret to keeping our kids from rebelling against their faith. They want to know what parenting formula we used to develop the amazing resilience Bethany showed in her comeback from tragic circumstances.

I am the first to say that it has only been by the grace of God that our kids turned out the way they have. I have a master child-rearing secret; it is called the Holy Bible. Its contents hold the greatest template to pattern our lives after. But upon reflection, and in talking about it with Tom and the kids, I do think there were some personal things we managed to get right. They were key things that helped contribute to how our kids have turned out.

The first key is that a healthy marriage makes for healthy families. I always thought that having a good marriage was the best gift I could give to our children. The value that Tom and I place on our relationship—our commitment to one another—is an anchor. This doesn't mean we don't get into squabbles from time to time, and we have had some rocky patches like anyone else; but our children always understood that we were committed to one another through thick and thin.

What is the secret to making our marriage work? God's Word! It teaches us to be slow to anger and quick to forgive. Jesus' words and His own example teach us that unconditional love and learning to die to our own selfishness is the way to live. The Scriptures say we shouldn't let the sun go down on our anger (see Eph. 4:26). I take seriously the idea that we must forgive each other and resolve conflict in a timely manner. Invariably this means that I have to be willing to forgive slights, whether they are perceived or real.

Another thing Tom and I managed to do was create boundaries for our kids that weren't so tight that they felt constricted and weren't so vague or loose that the boundaries were easily disregarded. We used God's Word to figure out what we would and would not permit; what standards we would maintain and what things were negotiable.

For example, we had boundaries about what kind of stuff we would watch on TV, or the kind of movies we would welcome into the house. Anything that promoted evil or was built on values totally contrary to what we were trying to communicate was discouraged. It didn't matter what other families were watching.

When the kids entered their teen years, I listened to the music they listened to as we drove to the beach. It was a great way to know the kind of music they enjoyed. The more I knew their tastes, the easier it was to find similar music for them that I knew, by my own research, had a positive message.

This actually worked pretty well because I had help from the church youth group they were a part of. It seemed that the best concerts on the island were the ones put on by the churches; so our kids naturally got attracted to music that was God-directed. Some really great rock bands formed from within the kids in the group who wanted to use their talent to honor God.

Above all, our kids understood that the boundaries we set were there because we loved them and because God loved them, and we wanted what was best for them, which is the same reason we disciplined them. "Discipline" is a word that scares a lot of people, including me, before I got to know and understand God's Word. I am a very undisciplined person with attention deficit challenges.

Tom and I learned the basics of successful marriage and parenting from Bible studies held at our church. We learned straight from the Owner's manual—the Holy Bible. We could trust what was being taught because it claimed to be of divine origin. There is plenty of evidence to back this claim. The 100-percent accuracy of thousands of years of prophecy and its proven fulfillment alone substantiate that the Bible could not have been written without divine inspiration and direction. The Bible teaches that Satan is alive and well and that he is the "Father of lies" (John 8:44). There is plenty of evidence on our planet and in our culture's media and advertising to confirm what the Bible teaches about Satan.

Hosea 4:6 says, "My people are destroyed from lack of knowledge." Our youth are living in a time when they face monumental challenges. The Bible is not called the Book of Life for nothing; the principles for living found in God's Word can give our children a hope and a future. But the simple fact is that children need to be given clear consequences for intentional boundary violations, like the time when I took Noah to the only Christian bookstore on the island at that time. I told Noah, who was three, that no, he could not get the card game he wanted, because I couldn't afford it, and it was for older kids. A few minutes later, I happened to glance over and see him slipping the cards into his pocket. I couldn't believe that my little three-year-old was stealing!

I took him right out into the hall and gave him a spanking before making him return the cards and apologize to the owner. He knew it was wrong, but in his heart he had decided that he wanted those cards more than he wanted to be obedient.

Like all parents, we had to use more creative methods to discipline our children as they grew older.

It seems that people all around you cuss without even knowing they're doing it; but of course, cussing was not suitable for the Hamilton household. If one of the boys said a cuss word, he would get a drop of hot sauce on his tongue. To show we didn't have a double standard, the punishment was the same for me.

I remember that at one point the kids were getting overly critical of one another, so I made a rule that before anyone in our family could say something critical or mean, he had to say 10 positive or affirming things. We live in a world where people are starved for a kind word. I hoped that by learning how to give compliments and encouragement, my children might bring life to people—just by their words of thoughtful kindness.

When one of the boys would put down or name-call his sibling or a friend, I would explain that, in a way, how he treated others is the way he also treats Christ. "I tell you the truth, when you did it to one of the least of these, my brothers and sisters, you were doing it to me!" (Matt. 25:40, NLT). So they had to apologize to Jesus as well as to the person they had insulted.

When the boys got rowdy on long drives to town, I'd pull over at a park or a road along the beach and let them run. This burned off a lot of energy and any aggressive edge, mellowing them out for the rest of the trip. Noah claims that I would let them get nearly to the van and then drive another quarter mile, but I think he's imagining that!

Sometimes as parents we try to make those magical moments called "quality time" happen on demand. For the most

Sisters Debbie and Cheri—future surfers ready for church!

Debbie and Cheri going snorkling for abalone with Dad at La Jolla Cove, California

Crawford High students Karin (Cheri's younger sister), Pam Falgren Riviera and Cheri

Cheri and Tom, 1979 (engagement photo)

Cheri surfing, 1979

Tom surfing the second reef of the Pipeline on the North Shore of Oahu, 1975

Tim (4), Noah (8) and Bethany (5 months) Cheri and Bethany

Hamilton family photo (photo by Steve Gnazzo, Kilohana Photography)

Bethany surfing, age 4

Bethany and Alana, two 7-year-olds (this was Bethany's first surfboard).

Bethany busted (she had just cut off her Barbie's hair)

Bethany and friends at Anini Beach

Bethany wins a surfboard (first place at the Rell Sunn Menehune Championships)

Bethany, always in the water, looking for fish and shells

Surf check with mom, always ready to film!

Bethany flying across the water

Happiness for the gift of life! (Cheri and Bethany in the hospital)

Prayer with Dad

Bethany's brother Timmy (18), dropping in on a big one (photo by Shea Sevilla)

Mike Coots and Bethany, two Kauai shark attack survivors

Bethany at the Louvre with Venus de Milo

Nick Vujicic and Bethany surfing

Bethany surfing—sun, rain or flooding!

Bethany surfing in Tahiti

Bethany with Sarah Hill at her 21st
birthday party

At the Kauai *Soul Surfer* premier with
Rick Bundschuh

Bethany's brother Noah surfing with power and style

Becky (Noah's wife) surfing without fear

The Hamilton movie family: Chris Brochu, Ross Thomas, Helen Hunt, Dennis Quaid, AnnaSophia Robb

Hana, the Hamilton's dog, surfing for the movie end credits

Cheri and Bethany at Focus on the Family in Colorado Springs, Colorado

The Hamiltons at the *Soul Surfer* premier: Tom, Cheri, Bethany, Timothy, Noah and Becky

part, quality time happens during long periods of quantity time. But what do you do when both parents have to work? More creative strategies . . . and a job that was a little different than something from 9 to 5.

I was blessed with a job delivering magazines to kiosks and stands all over the island. Tom was usually working nights and surfing during the days, so I loaded up our van with magazines and little Bethany and headed out. The boys were in school, but I could be back in time to take them all to the beach. There was no time clock for me to punch or deadline for the magazines to be delivered other than by the end of the day.

We could take a break and stop anywhere along the way to enjoy a playground, visit animals at the Humane Society or have lunch on the beach. When the kids were older and began surfing, I would deliver magazines in the summer while they would enjoy a surf session on the other side of the island. Sure, this adventure-filled delivery schedule always took a lot longer, but with the boys and even Bethany helping me load the magazine racks, the work part went by quickly.

The deeper blessing about my magazine delivery job was that it was my personal Bible and spiritual education time. If the kids stayed home with Tom, I would use my alone time to pray and worship God as I played my Christian music and learn from Bible studies on the car radio and CDs played on my car stereo. A full delivery route could take eight hours, more or less, depending on how much work I could fit in the schedule with everything else going on, namely surf.

Somewhere over the rainbow is a constant reality on Kauai! It is raining hard right now, and I am thinking about where I could go to get dry. Usually, if we are on the North Shore of Kauai, we could go to town and get dry. It can rain for weeks here, but we get used to it and learn to strategize our life around it. We save our town trips with a movie for the really bad weather days, that is, if our windshield wipers work.

We have warm, balmy, soft trade winds that come in from the southeast and push the clouds up onto the mountains above Hanalei Bay, and then the rain dumps into the valley. These are predictable and consistent rains, nurturing the taro and the wetlands of the North Shore. And oh, the wet, green beautiful valleys filled with rainbows and waterfalls!

When we are really desperate to get away from the rain, we head to Polihale. This beach is the official beach, seriously, at the end of the rainbow. Hot, dry, dusty miles of bumpy road lead to the reward of a soft, sandy white beach filled with roaring dangerous surf, to our camera's delight. Kauai is 30 miles wide by 60 miles long, and the highway is along the ocean, ending at Polihale, with the other end at Ke'e Lagoon—Ke'e being the safest place to swim and snorkel, and Polihale being the most dangerous, with rips that will sweep you off your feet in seconds.

Kauai has more bridges to cross than any place else per square foot because it has more rain, which equals more sand washing down to the ocean from more rivers and more riverbeds to create and maintain more beaches. So, if you don't mind crossing bridges, you can enjoy the beautiful beaches; and if you look back from where you've come, you can see more rainbows than you have ever seen before.

Kayaking was and is an adventure we try to do every summer. A family friend told me the following story about one such kayaking trip:

"Dig . . . keep your head down!" I shouted in encouragement to my son David. He manned the front of a two-man kayak as we strained, trying to paddle directly into the wind and waves. A couple of hundred yards ahead I could catch glimpses of Tom's and Bethany's heads bobbing in the water by their overturned kayak. A few hundred feet to our right were the inaccessible Na Pali cliffs stretching into the distance in both directions. The wind and swell had been building fast and now surged 10 to 20 feet against the cliff face and bounced back at us. Slowly, we gained on the two figures struggling in the water ahead of us.

We had left the beachhead at Ke'e barely an hour earlier on a beautiful, calm morning. Now the wind was howling and white caps were breaking over us. Tom had shown up at our rendezvous point with a then eight-year-old Bethany and an open two-man kayak. By "open," I mean open-hulled or "sinkable." Also with us were Tom's son Timmy, then 12, and my son Logan, the same age, piloting single kayaks. My 10-year-old son, David, and I rounded out the expedition in an unsinkable two-man kayak. We were off to paddle 12-plus miles and camp out for a couple of nights.

I explained that taking an 8-year-old girl and having an open kayak were not good ideas, but Tom said it was fine. I love that about Tom. You don't have to waste time discussing things, because he's not going to change his mind. So, we took off on an adventure.

The wind and waves were behind us and kept rising as we made our way down the infamous Na Pali coast. The boys and I reached the first sea cave. It was about 300 feet long and came out on the other side of a point.

We decided to risk the rising swell and were able to ride a wave right on through. It's a super rush as the wave jacks up and you swear you're going to be scraped along the ceiling. Once out, you take a hard right and exit into a choppy but sheltered cove behind the point.

We waited and waited, but no Tom. Eventually, I told Logan and Timmy to go on slowly ahead while David and I paddled back around the outside of the point to check on Tom and Bethany. As soon as we rounded the point, the wind hit us with unbelievable force. Far behind we saw Tom and Bethany in the water with a sinking kayak. Now we had to battle our way back against the wind and the current. By the time we got to them, we had to paddle full bore just to stay beside them. Tom asked me to take Bethany in my kayak and said he would stay with the boat. Not a great plan, but this wasn't the time to have a discussion.

In seconds, Bethany was in our boat, and the wind and waves took us away. By the time I looked back, Tom was already a couple hundred feet behind and almost lost among the spray and swells. But then, as I looked again—a miracle—the first boat we'd seen, a catamaran tour boat, was heading toward Tom from the ocean side. This boat had a big open deck and carried up to 25 passengers. The last thing I saw as we ran with the seas was people trying to wrestle the kayak onto their boat. Tom's last words, echoed in my mind, were "see you in Kalalau."

Our plan was to break our trip into three parts while doing some exploring along the way. We were about halfway to our first stop, the Kalalau Valley, a wide beautiful place with beaches, rivers and waterfalls. It used to be home for more than 5,000 Hawaiians, but now it has reverted to nature with only goats, pigs, and campers on the beach . . . and, well, also quite a few usually naked hippies in hidden camps.

The next miles were relatively uneventful and almost peaceful as we got away from the turbulence of the cliffs. We caught up with Timmy and Logan and had a chance to appreciate the spectacular scenery rising thousands of feet above us. Miles ahead we could see the beach at Kalalau.

Meanwhile, Tom had emptied his open kayak and, despite the loud protests of the passengers, took off in pursuit of us. Tom said that the captain, a fellow surfer, assured everyone that he could handle the rugged conditions, but then Tom has been known to minimize danger. He did admit later, amusedly, that one poor woman was weeping hysterically and begging the captain not to let him back in the water because he was going to die. Personally, I doubt if the captain could have stopped him!

With less than a mile to go, we approached the beach where we would land. Between us and our destination, however, was the Kalalau River mouth, which left the water shallow far off shore. As we looked out to sea, a huge set of waves started to plough across the ocean between the beach and us. We slowed down to assess the situation. The safest thing to do was to head a half-mile out to sea and go around the reef. We watched and judged the time between sets. It seemed we could shoot across to the beach, if luck held.

As the last wave of the set came through, we were already charging it. Halfway across the distance, Logan and Timmy were doing well. There were no waves in sight and I thought that we were safe. Just then, Bethany, who was sitting in the bow facing me, opened her eyes very wide. She pointed and yelled, "Mr. Miles!" I turned to look over my shoulder and saw a 10-foot wave face start to curl and break behind us.

I immediately went down on my back and dug in the paddle, pulling us around to run with the wave. We were up in the air, then racing down the face. "Just catching a wave," I said through clenched teeth to calm Bethany's fears (and mine). My whole strength was on the paddle to keep us on the wave. I still remember Bethany's face turning from terror to joy as we rode and rode that wave. This went on for a quarter- to half-mile—certainly the longest ride I've ever had on a kayak.

When the wave finally weakened and slid beneath us, we saw that the beach was just a few hundred feet in front of us. We would still have to brave a huge beach break, get rolled around, lose and retrieve our food and camping gear, but we had made it! And half an hour later there came Tom . . . no worries!

After this, we took a shower in a cool freshwater waterfall, hiked, camped, cooked over a fire, saw a turtle lay eggs at night, and looked at the incredible stars as we slept out on the sand. Good times and long days lazing in the shade.

We began the last leg out with much calmer seas in the lea of the island. We had to paddle much harder now, as there was less wind. However, it was still rough enough to where Tom suddenly sunk again, so we paddled over to again pick up Bethany. Tom wanted to stay with the boat (déjà vu), and this time the conditions were not so bad and we were on a section of coast that usually had more boats coming and going. So we left, paddling the last two miles to land at Polihale Beach. We pulled our kayaks out of the water and onto the dunes, where someone was to soon meet us to drive us back around the island. We sat and waited for Tom . . . and waited . . . and waited.

Finally, we spotted something odd out in the water that wasn't a boat. Slowly, it became more visible. It was, in fact, Tom. He had rigged up some ropes into a harness and was swimming the last two miles dragging the overturned two-man kayak full of water . . . no worries. As he came closer, we jumped in the surf to help bring the boat through the five- to six-foot shore break.

As it turns out, a kayak with 500 gallons of water can really knock you around. It rolled in the waves, it rolled in the sand, and it rolled on us. Some four-wheel drive trucks with a dozen local guys had pulled up on the beach about a hundred feet from us and were having a good time drinking beer until we started kayak wrestling in the surf. Now they were having a hilarious time . . . laughing at us. I would tend to ignore a beer-drinking crowd in this situation, but not Tom. He strode over there and yelled, "What's wrong with you guys? Can't you see we need help?" They looked at each other, they looked at their feet, and then jumped down and got in the surf. Before you knew it, we were back on the beach, a mollified Tom, a rescued kayak, and being offered a beer . . . no worries.

While we were not one of those families with traditions, we tried to build memories together by doing simple things, usually on the beach. Birthday parties were always on the beach with a mom-made piñata of papier mâché. On Christmas morning, forget about opening presents. A morning surf session came first on the agenda, and then family gifts were opened while enjoying a late breakfast.

Most of all, Tom and I realized that our own faith had to be genuine and alive every day. You can tell kids what to do all day, but more is caught than taught. What we do weighs 10 times more than anything we say.

It was good that I was learning all of these parenting truths, because after eight years of learning the ropes with two rambunctious boys, Bethany was born in February 1990. I finally had a girl!

CHAPTER

8

Hopes, Dreams and Hurricanes

The name of the LORD is a strong fortress;
the godly run to it and are safe.

PROVERBS 18:10, *NLT*

We had two boys, and I had settled into motherhood. I was already locked into my future as a shuttle driver to surf spots and sporting events. I was happy, no doubt about it; but I was determined to have a girl. I used to tell Tom, "We are going to keep having kids until there's another female in the family!"

Working late nights can hinder your sex life. On a rare night off, Tom and I enjoyed a romantic evening. The next morning at the market, I bumped into a good friend. Out of nowhere, Karin said, "Cheri, you are going to have a baby girl."

I believed that God had spoken a word of knowledge through Karin as taught in 1 Corinthians 12:8 and illustrated in the story where Mary first visits her cousin Elizabeth, who receives the word of knowledge about the baby that Mary was carrying (see Luke 1:41-42).

In fact, I was so certain that I was having a girl that I never picked out a boy's name. Immediately believing, and while reading the Bible, I chose the name "Bethany," because I read it was the hometown of Mary, Martha and Lazarus, as well as the place where Jesus raised Lazarus from the dead; and I loved how "Bethany" sounded. Tom got to pick the middle name, and he chose Meilani—Hawaiian for "Heavenly Flower."

The boys were already accomplished junior watermen. I could only pray that Bethany would find the same kind of joy in the ocean that we did, and still do. No need to worry . . . she was born with saltwater in her veins and took to the ocean like a fish.

By the time Bethany was born, Noah was an active eight-year-old and Timmy was getting ready to start school. Tom and I were juggling our schedules at the hotel that had gone through yet another expensive renovation. Things were always tight financially, but we lived carefully, which today is called going green.

After two years in the river house behind the Dolphin restaurant in Hanalei, we had to move out. It was a sad day, as we had enjoyed kayaking and watching Noah fish for Tilapia.

I always called upon the Lord in prayer when we moved; where you live can greatly influence your children's lives because of safety issues and the friends that influence them. So it was important to ask for wisdom from above.

One late afternoon, my two sons and I were on our way to take dinner to one of my good friends from church who had recently given birth. The whole church was providing meals, and it was our turn. At about 5:00 P.M., as the boys and I were on our way to Claudia's house, we saw a triple rainbow. The Hawaiians believe that when you see a sign in the heavens, something special is happening!

That night, Tom and I stayed up late. About 11:00 P.M., my water broke. I packed a bag of items to take to the hospital and then decided to clean the bathroom because it's so nice to have a really clean bathroom with a new baby. I asked Tom to call the hospital and let them know we were coming in. By 1:00 A.M., my labor was getting more intense, so I said we needed to leave *now!* It takes about an hour to get to the hospital from the North Shore. Tom does not mind driving fast, so we made good time on the empty highway. I had to turn up the stereo full blast when the labor pains got too intense. I knew I was dilating, and I was thinking about how fast Timmy had been born . . . a short two hours.

We entered the emergency room at almost 2:00 A.M., where I was put on a wheeled bed behind a curtain. The doctor took one quick look and went to prep a few things. Of course, as soon as he was gone, Bethany arrived at 2:10 A.M.—early, fast and beautiful!

On November 11, 1992, Hurricane Iniki slammed into Kauai dead-on. The eye of the storm passed directly over us and the destructive 145-mile-per-hour winds leveled whole neighborhoods.

In the days leading up to the most powerful hurricane to hit the islands in recorded history, everyone was simply going about their business. Tom and I had left the kids with a friend the day before and headed to the other side of the island to catch some truly amazing surf. We enjoyed a glorious day with blue skies and perfect waves, a day we will always remember.

The next morning, we woke up before dawn. I decided it was too rainy and windy and thought that for me it was a better day to stay home with the kids. Tom thought the waves were too good to pass up just because of a little bad weather, so he said goodbye and jumped into the van for the long trek to the other side of the island. By the time he got to the nearest town, he knew something was wrong. Lines of cars snaked out from every gas station. People were gathered in front of the stores, waiting for them to open.

Tom turned on the radio and pulled over as the news washed over him. He heard that a hurricane watch had become a full hurricane warning; destruction was imminent. Tom found a store that had just opened and managed to pick up some provisions, miraculously before the crowds descended. The sirens went off at first light and I became aware that this was not just a heavy rainstorm. Tom raced back home to help us prepare for the impending disaster.

We both still had strong memories of Hurricane Iwa, which had passed within 25 miles of Kauai, in 1982. That had only been a Category 1 hurricane, but it had devastated the island, flattening the predominately tin-roofed, single-panel walled houses and creating huge storm surges that carried boats and cars across the coastal lowlands.

We took one look at our old-style plantation-era home and decided that we'd better find somewhere else to take shelter. The neighbors across the street had a solid, stone-built house, and they welcomed us to join them. Tom and I gathered up the kids and left the laundry on the line as the winds started to pick up outside.

The first thing I noticed was the smell.

As the increasing wind stripped the leaves from the trees and foliage everywhere was torn up and scattered, there came the pungent scent of newly mown grass. Trees were uprooted and covered the road. Then began the bombardment upon the house from untold debris and shingles from the neighbors' roofs. By this time the wind was whistling and howling like a freight train and we could barely hear one another speak unless we shouted.

I, perhaps foolishly, wasn't really that scared. I was more curious to know what was happening to our house across the street, so I crept up and peeked out the window. Every tree was bent over, straining in the wind. Sheets of rain and wreckage swirled around like crazed bats; but I could still see the laundry I'd left on the line; it was literally standing out straight and totally horizontal.

A few of the others joined me, and we watched the storm in awe. That is, until, with a rending sound, we saw the garage roof belonging to the house we were sheltering in go flying up and over us.

After hours of tense waiting, and watching the houses around us disintegrate, there came a sudden calm. The eye of the hurricane was directly over us and everything was quiet and still. We all walked outside, and for the first time we could see the incredible damage around us. The homes of our neighbors and friends were roofless or in pieces; some homes had simply vanished. As we surveyed the destruction, we were surprised to see that our house had survived, but Noah's bedroom was missing.

By early evening the storm had passed and the sun set behind the once lush, green mountains. The Garden Island was ravaged—trees denuded, livestock and agriculture devastated, beaches radically altered and covered in churned-up debris. The roads were impassable, and nearly every power line down. Within minutes, every neighbor with a chainsaw began working to clear the roads.

We took off in our van with the video camera rolling to document some of the damage and check on friends. Stopping at the Hanalei Valley Lookout, I saw the exact mountainside I had seen in a vivid dream two months earlier that had lost all its foliage. I believe it was a supernatural dream from God. Other Christians had also had dreams and prophetic words. I remembered the prophecy I heard three months earlier that said, "The eye of the storm would pass over Kauai."

The water pumps had gone down with the loss of electricity. Not having water was the biggest challenge. You couldn't flush your toilet! I had filled up our bathtub and a few other buckets of water, so we were able to make our toilet work sparingly.

It was extraordinarily hot after the storm passed, so we headed to the closest waterfall for a shower. Of course, almost everyone else in the neighborhood had the same idea, so there was already a line in front of the beautiful, refreshing waterfall.

There was no electricity, no stores or gas stations to go to, no work except to try to patch together what shelter and subsistence could be scrounged up for yourself or your neighbor. The economy was wrecked. Tourists fled, hotels were shuttered, first flights out of the island were packed with people escaping back to the mainland, forever telling of their nightmare vacation on Kauai. The storm had destroyed our church building and scattered our church family into other churches around the island.

In addition, Tom had parked our van in the parking lot of the nearby elementary school, logically thinking that it would be safe from falling trees or buildings. We'd only bought the van—our first new car—in 1988. We were determined to keep this one in good shape. But we didn't count on the fact that huge pieces of the school would tear off and sail into the parking lot. We don't know what part of the building smacked into our car, but it was more than just dented here and there. It had even been spun 180 degrees by wind and whatever else hit it.

Our insurance company declared the van totaled and gave us a check for $11,500. This was all we had, along with unemployment money, to survive on for the next year. We were thankful that the van was still drivable; but with all the debris, including ample amounts of roofing nails, scattered along the road, flat tires were a constant occurrence for everyone navigating the roadways.

When we tried to make a repair reservation to get the van worked on, we were told it would be a six-month wait! We decided to ship the van to Oahu and have the bodywork and repainting done there. We chose blue, like the ocean, for the repaint. It only took two weeks. We enjoyed a few days of vacation on Oahu, then drove our blue beach cruiser to the docks and shipped it home.

With no income, we wondered how we'd be able to pay the mortgage on the lot we'd owned for 10 years. We had approved plans and soon planned to build; when we lost our jobs, the bank tried to foreclose. But with the island's financial infrastructure wiped out as well, the government put a moratorium on all mortgages.

Of course, Bethany was too little to remember any of this, but Noah and Timmy both have lots of adventure stories about life after the hurricane. The military set up a base camp right in the Princeville Park. They flew in daily helicopters supplied with MREs (Meals Ready to Eat). Each day different items showed up at the 5:00 P.M. drop—water bottles, ice, tarps, lights . . . always something different. It was just like a "Mash Camp." You could stay, or go through the food line for some fresh army gourmet!

It took almost a year for life to return to normal. The Weston Hotel where we had worked had been sold to the Marriot for a rock bottom price of $50 million. The hotel then had to undergo post-hurricane refurbishment, which probably cost as much as the initial price. The Marriot was not hiring back those of us who were union, so both Tom and I had to look elsewhere for work. Tom fought them for six months, writing letters and making phone calls, trying to get his job back. They should have hired him just for his tenacity!

I called a friend from church who owned the Menu Magazine and asked for the job delivering visitor brochures and magazines across the island. This helped our family get back into a good rhythm that would carry us along for the next few years.

Money was always tight, but surf was good, and God's hand was there for us.

As our kids matured, their distinct personalities flourished in their own healthy and vigorous ways, while developing their own walk with God.

Noah was our intense and serious child. His favorite movie was *Inspector Gadget* and his favorite TV show was *MacGyver*. I taught him to safely change his first tire when he was only seven years old. He started getting involved in church more during junior high and went to church youth camps and activities. Many of his friends started taking their first steps toward a relationship with Christ as well.

Noah embraced the paintball rage and would disappear into the nearby jungle with his friends, only to reappear dirty and sweaty in the afternoon to compare battle-wound welts. Tom and I passed on our interest in photography to our children. In sixth grade, at Kilauea School, Noah won a state honor for the picture he took of the original Hanalei Post Office, and he won a trip to Oahu.

These two factors may have kick-started Noah toward a career in photography. He developed a talent for taking photos of his friends surfing. It turns out that Noah also has a good nose for business, and we turned over to him the daunting role of managing the family interests and concerns in all things having to do with Bethany's surfing career. He also shoots all of Bethany's official photos.

Our second son, Timmy, is Noah's opposite in many ways. Laid back and relaxed, yet possessing a wry and oddball sense of humor, Tim jokes that he grew up being "Noah's brother" until

Bethany's shark attack put her on the front pages. Then he went to being "Bethany's brother."

One of the things I got involved in early on was a public school release-time program with my long-time friend Barbara Tofte, where kids got an excused absence an hour a week for religious instruction. Because people were touchy about church and state separation, parents had to sign a waiver for kids to participate. To our amazement, lots of parents did.

I was a teacher's aide to Barbara, and we were able to use that time to share Christ with a group of North Shore kids. It was after one of those classes (where I had to teach the class for Barbara because she was ill) that I had the wonderful opportunity to lead my own son Timmy to faith in Christ.

Barbara had called me at the last minute and said that I'd have to teach the whole class by myself, so I only had time to grab a music video by Christian recording artist Michael W. Smith that told a powerful story about Jesus dying on the cross. On the way home, Timmy, who had recently come close to drowning, asked how he could be sure that he would go to heaven.

For all of his usual playful manner, I could tell that he was very serious, and so we talked about the music video, which compared the difference between heaven and hell. Finally, I just pulled the van off the road and led him in a prayer of faith, asking for forgiveness of sin and inviting Jesus into his little heart to be his Lord and Savior. There is nothing better for a Christian mother than a life-changing event like that!

Tim carved out his own unique personality while sandwiched between two over-the-top siblings. It was Timmy who decided that he would rather bodyboard than stand-up surf, making him the odd one out among the rest of his surfing family. Timmy also got into shooting videos, almost exclusively of his fellow bodyboarders, and then editing them into hour-long movies with no real plot, just great footage and rocking music. He worked alongside guys such as Bob Sato, manager of the Kauai Classic Bodyboard Team.

Also, Timmy is the mischief-maker; if something zany was going on, you could bank on him being right in the middle of it. After camping high in the mountains of Kauai, Tim and some friends decided they wanted to descend the steep, winding 15-mile road on a mattress—an unusual vehicle no matter which way you slice it.

The boys put skateboard wheels on a wooden frame and then tossed an old mattress on it; they called it a "bed sled." Tim and his longtime friend Pypyr piled onto the mattress and took off down the hill, using their weight to bank the steep turns and dragging the edge of the mattress against the asphalt to brake. Meanwhile, another friend followed in a car so that no one would run them over from behind.

Of course, all the kids got into some sort of mischief—like the common trick of "pool-hopping," where they and their friends would go from one hotel pool to another, trying to stay ahead of the security guards who were valiantly attempting to keep the pools reserved for tourists and guests only. Not to mention that the security guards knew all the kids by sight.

These were the kind of antics that were hard for us to get upset about when we heard about them, especially considering *our* past.

Later, all of our children were active with the youth group at North Shore Christian Church (nicknamed The Tent Church, because we met under a large tent), which was doing some really wonderful things, such as mission trips to orphanages. On top of being regulars at midweek Bible studies, the kids helped out as staff during youth camps for the younger kids.

Because Scripture memorization is key to promoting spiritual growth, we found that one of the best ways to memorize God's Word is through music. God's Word can help you and your children get through difficult times, guide and direct, correct and help keep you from harm. We learned so many Scripture songs in church and through children's music videos and DVDs.

On a town trip with the kids, I parked the car in an empty parking lot, and when I came back, someone had parked their car blocking me in. It was an outrage, and I got upset. I thought about letting the air out of that car's tires! As the kids waited to see what I would do about it, I remembered the words of the Scripture song we were listening to from Romans 12:21: "Do not be overcome by evil, but overcome evil with good" (*NIV*). I decided to honor God and not let my sinful nature rule the day. We got into the car and I had to drive over the sidewalk in order to leave.

In addition to church and surfing, our kids were involved in many sports. Soccer and swimming were big with all of our kids. Timmy, in particular, demonstrated a natural ability in just about any sport he tackled; and both of the boys were pretty good at the quick-moving sport of roller hockey.

Having a girl to raise was different than raising two boys, but I pretty much stuck to the same format. I encouraged the kids in all their team sports, because it helped them work together, make friends and establish good, healthy relationships built around activities instead of hanging out at a mall or something else.

As with both boys, we wanted to give Bethany swimming lessons at an early age, but since we couldn't afford them, I taught her myself. Before long, she was on the local swim team. Soon she was winning swim meets in her age division.

Being on swim team also helped our kids build their endurance in the water. By the time she was seven, Bethany could swim a mile without getting exhausted. This would come in very handy as she started to surf larger waves farther from shore.

Of course, there was the surfing, surfing, and more surfing!

The local surf shop in Hanalei started a surf team. Charlie Cowden, the owner, hired Russell Lewis as coach and opened the team free of charge to the young kids who would commit to Coach's training regimen.

Seven-year-old Bethany and her friend Alana signed right up. They were given a nice discount at the surf shop, loaded up with stickers and T-shirts and then put to drilling exercises in between surf sessions. On a team of all boys, they were the only girls.

The combination of swim team and surf team really pushed the girls' endurance, confidence and skill level; before long they were winning surf contests, alternating between first and second place. Within a few years, it was apparent that Bethany had a shot at being a professional surfer. When I was young, being a pro surfer meant some clothes and maybe a small check if you managed to win a surf contest. Today the sport is fueled by corporations offering winning purses, and by sponsors offering salaries to the top-ranking surfers on their rosters.

Women's surfing, while still not as lucrative as men's, is far removed from the stereotypes of beach-betty eye-candy. Any girl talented enough to make it up the ladder in ratings can earn a fair living being a professional surfer. Motivated and encouraged by her equally talented friend Alana, Bethany became a hard-charging fixture around Kauai, dropping in on waves that even surfers years older considered good-sized. When she was still in grade school, we started to travel so that she could compete in the local junior contests on the other islands.

I remember the night when Tom and I sat down and talked about schooling options for our daughter. It seemed that her God-given talent was taking her in a direction that would make typical school unworkable, particularly as her competition schedule and training took place during normal school hours. We decided to enroll her in school courses online. Alana did the same thing; so they each kept their closest surf and training partner. As friends, they strategized, using the same game plan so they could fast-track their surfing careers together.

By the time Bethany was 13, she had a solid track record in junior surfing competition. It couldn't have come at a better time, because the boys were getting established and independent. Noah had graduated, finished his two years at Heald Business College and was entering into his photography career; Timmy was finishing up high school and looking toward the future. Now my focus could go primarily to Bethany. I became her surf mom and coach, her cheering section, cook, chauffeur and laundry maid. I even videoed her surf sessions so we could critique her later. She managed to get picked up by Rip Curl, which was an important help.

The rest of the family helped Bethany's blossoming surf career too. It was Timmy who encouraged her to paddle into bigger waves. It was Tom and I who shot hours and hours of video, and Noah took hundreds of photos of her. Nothing makes you learn to surf better than watching yourself to catch and correct mistakes and bad habits.

The prospect of 13-year-old Bethany becoming a professional surfer before she was out of high school was getting brighter. A surfing career, as a believer in Jesus Christ, should not simply be a means for gaining money, trophies or accolades, but a way to give glory to God. I remember that Bethany and I prayed about this very thing several weeks before she was attacked. Our prayer went like this: *Lord, bring Bethany into the center of Your will and use her surfing to glorify and honor Your name.* It never occurred to us the manner in which God would answer our prayer.

This was a time when our lives had a familiar routine. I'd wake up early, check the surf report and then rouse Bethany to let her know where we might find the best surf. After drinking a quick smoothie, we'd load up our surf van, pick up Alana and then go off to find waves. I would video the girls and get them home by 10:00 A.M. to get the schoolwork started. We then put in a quick afternoon surf session. After dinner, we would watch the video so they could evaluate their performance.

I had never lost the desire to seriously get back into surfing. Ever since Noah's birth, I'd put my passion aside. Now I decided that this might be the time to get back on the board. In my mind's eye, I could see myself surfing waves with the girls. Now that would be awesome!

But first I'd need to get back into shape.

Surfing any waves demands strength and endurance. You have to be able to take a punishing wipeout, hold your breath under the crush of gallons of water, and paddle to keep yourself in the surging lineup. I was a long way from my physical prime, but I knew that I had the discipline and motivation to stick to training. I decided that I would get into the local swim club and start working out every day. I dug out my racing-style swimsuit and goggles, picked up some earplugs and packed them and a towel into my beach bag, ready for the day.

I was excited. In a few weeks, if I worked hard, I'd be able to join Noah, Timmy, Bethany and her friends out in the lineup as the winter waves started to arrive. Of course, Tom, would be out there too.

I glanced at the calendar and was reminded that it was October 31. I would drop Bethany off at the beach for some surfing, come home and grab my swim gear and head to the pool for my long-overdue workout regimen. It was a great day to start on my dreams.

Except that things often do not go as planned.

CHAPTER

9

In the Shadow of Death

You intended to harm me, but God intended it for good to accomplish what is now being done, the saving of many lives.

GENESIS 50:20, *NIV*

It was late Thursday afternoon after our thrift shop venture to get Halloween costumes when I took Alana and Bethany to a surf break called Tunnels. It was the first place I ever surfed on Kauai. We had just checked another spot that looked really fun, but it was too crowded and didn't have enough waves for the guys already out there. So we ended up at Tunnels.

That day there were small waves coming in off the corner of the reef, with glassy conditions, the wind being almost nonexistent. By now it was 5:00 P.M. I told the girls they could paddle out for a few waves while I read a book on the beach. What none of us knew was that a shark had been harassing the surfers who had just come in. If we had known that, we would have changed our plans right then and also the next morning.

When the girls reached the lineup, a freak storm showed up out of nowhere, blowing the little waves apart and pelting us all with rain. I ran for cover under the trees as the girls paddled back to the beach without catching a single wave. I sometimes wonder if that storm was part of God's providence to avoid something from happening when there would have been no one out there in the water to help them.

On Friday, the next morning, I realized it was going to be a full day. The girls were older and stronger now and would soon be surfing the powerful outer reef breaks too far out for me to film. I had my beach bag ready to go swim after I took them surfing. I needed to work up to 60 laps in the pool without feeling exhausted if I was going to surf again and keep up with the heavier stuff the kids were now paddling into.

Timmy was eating breakfast, but Tom was fasting because he was heading to the hospital for an operation on his knee (he had torn his meniscus cartilage while surfing a few years ago, and he'd recently tweaked it again). After he dropped his dad off at the hospital, Timmy was heading off to Kapaa High School.

Tonight was October 31, Halloween 2003. Thirteen-year-old Bethany and Alana had their costumes ready for this evening's fun. She and Alana had scoured the Kilauea thrift store and had each scored matching "men in black" outfits of suit, loafer shoes, hat and sunglasses. The girls would first go to a Fall Festival at our church with Sarah Hill before cruising with friends all over the neighborhood trick-or-treating.

I checked the surf report.

October is an odd month because the swells are shifting from a southern to a northern direction, occasionally firing off from both directions at once. The surf report wasn't very hopeful, but part of the duty of a professional surfer is learning to shred in little mushy waves, which is usually all you have to work with during a contest. You can predict waves all you want, but they don't always show up the morning of a contest.

As was our ritual, Ginger, our dog, helped me roust Bethany. "Wake up," I said. "Let's go check the surf."

My job that morning was chauffeur. I also would video surf sessions if the waves were worthy. We had our van, which we nicknamed the "Blue Crush." It was ugly, but it was perfect for all the sand, wax, wet towels and bathing suits, not to mention how many extra kids and surfboards we could fit into it.

At Wilcox Hospital, Tom wasn't looking forward to his surgery, but because this was the second repair job on his knee, he thought it would be interesting to watch the surgery, so he opted for a spinal tap rather than full anesthesia. Bethany was taking her sweet time getting ready, so I made her a bowl of Raisin Bran to go as we drove to look for waves. We called Alana to see if she wanted to join us; but unlike Bethany, Alana's not much of an early riser. Like us, the Blanchards are a dedicated surfing family with a similar routine and would not be far behind after they dropped Alana's little brother off at Hanalei School.

The sun was just cracking over the horizon as we drove down the hill on our surf check. The view of the bay as you weave down the road leading into Hanalei is spectacular. The bay looked flat with no white water lines showing breaking waves.

Instead of calling it quits, we decided to go all the way to the end of the road. You never know when one of the other spots will have a little something to surf.

After an unsuccessful search, Bethany was resigned to go home and start her online schoolwork. On the way back home, we spotted Alana, her dad, Holt, and her brother Byron. They had just pulled into Tunnels parking lot to check the surf.

"Hey, there's some surf," they said. "It's small, but . . ."

It was tiny out, but the prospect of surfing with Alana rather than doing schoolwork excited Bethany. "Can I stay with them?" she asked me.

"We'll probably only surf for an hour," Holt said. "I'll drop her off when we're done."

I figured it would take me just a few extra minutes to grab my swim bag and get to the pool, so I said enthusiastically, "Great!"

Bethany was already getting her board and towel out of the van.

As I turned around and drove off, I noticed Jeff Walba waxing his board. Jeff was a North Shore regular who had been off island for a while. I remember thinking, *Gee, I haven't seen that guy for years.* But there was no time to play catch-up; I was off to begin training for my long-deferred return to surfing.

It was already about 7:30 A.M. when I got home and grabbed my gear. I was almost out the door when the phone rang. I thought about not answering it, as I was on a mission; but then the thought occurred to me that it might be Bethany wanting a ride home, so I glanced down. I was puzzled when the caller ID said it was Jeff Walba calling me.

What could he possibly want? I thought, as I picked up the receiver.

I will never forget his words. "Cheri, there's been an accident. You need to go to the hospital. Your daughter has been attacked by a shark."

My first impulse was that this was some joke of Bethany's and that she would grab the phone and say, "Okay, you can come get me, I need a ride home."

So I said, "Come on, what's really going on?"

Jeff, no doubt taken aback by my response, got very serious and with a tight voice said, "No, really, she's been attacked by a shark."

My adrenaline exploded!

As I woke Noah, I screamed, "We've got to go to the hospital, Bethany's been attacked by a shark."

"What happened?" He was groggy, trying to understand. Then he wanted answers, details. But I didn't know anything.

The phone rang again. This time it was the police who reported to me that my daughter had been attacked by a shark and was heading to the hospital in an ambulance. I asked the officer what her condition was, but he replied that he was not permitted to give any more information.

After packing clothes into an overnight bag, enough for a few days in the hospital, I made a quick call to the *700 Club* and asked for prayer. Then I bolted out the door. I didn't wait for Noah as he made a call to Sarah Hill.

What happened on that fateful Halloween morning has been told many times and is covered in Bethany's book and the *Soul Surfer* film. But just in case, let me give a brief outline. Four surfers, Holt, Byron, Alana and Bethany, paddled out for 10 minutes to surf the waves at Tunnels. I headed home to my swim workout at a nearby pool. Tunnels is an outer reef that sits almost a quarter mile off shore in deep water.

Everyone knew that it would be a short session, just a light workout to enjoy the morning sun and the small but clean-breaking waves. Bethany had only caught one or two waves and was now lying on her surfboard, dangling her arm in the blue sparkly water as she quietly waited for a wave to come her way. She was just a few yards from Alana when she felt a jiggle, jiggle, tug on her left arm. Looking back over her shoulder and out of the corner of her eye, she caught a gray blur slipping back in the water from where it came.

In a hauntingly calm voice, she called to Alana, but loud enough for everyone to hear, "I've just been attacked by a shark." The attack was silent and quick; but in that split second the shark had taken off her arm near the shoulder, leaving a huge jaw-shaped crescent bite mark on her surfboard.

The Blanchards were momentarily paralyzed, and then Holt went into action. He saw a small wave coming and told Bethany "You're going in!" and he pushed her into the wave as she lay on her board. Byron caught the same wave and rode alongside her while Alana and Holt caught the following wave.

They quickly caught up and helped Byron pull Bethany, on her surfboard, over the remainder of the reef. The waves had taken them partway over the shallow reef, and then they had to scramble the rest of the way to the end of the jagged rock island. Byron switched his board with Bethany's so she would float better the remaining distance to the shore.

Holt, with a raised voice, commanded Byron, "Go ahead! Call 911, don't wait for us!" Byron then raced to the beach and ran to the truck to call 911. Holt, in the meantime, had removed his surf shirt to tie around the remaining portion of Bethany's severed arm as a makeshift tourniquet.

He then said to Bethany, "Hold on to my surf trunks and don't let go, Bethany." He rallied Alana to paddle alongside Bethany and keep her on board physically and mentally. Alana paddled close to her, knowing that there was an awful lot of blood in the water. Alana was choking back sobs as she struggled with the dire situation. The long paddle back to the beach over the dark deep channel did not feel safe to any of them as they towed Bethany to shore.

Meanwhile, Byron didn't have the keys to their truck, so he had to break the window to reach the cell phone. Alana took a few moments to throw up on the beach as soon as she got to shore. And a lady visitor ran to her nearby vacation rental to get her husband, a paramedic, who rushed to the beach to help out the moment Bethany came in from the water.

Once on shore, Bethany was laid on her back on the surf-board while Holt replaced the surf shirt tourniquet with a surf leash that held firm with its strong Velcro seal. A little dog wandered onto the scene and peered into Bethany's white face, perking her up. Someone called out, "Get the lifeguard!" Bethany was the one who informed them that no one was on duty this early.

The paramedic said that Holt did an excellent job with the leash after inspecting the wound area. Then Bethany was carried on the surfboard that was used like a stretcher to the back of Holt's truck.

Emergency crews were already racing to Tunnels as Jeff Walba, still at the beach, became the first one to contact me. He must have gotten my number from Holt or Alana.

There are some crucial things—some would say coincidences—that came together to save Bethany on that life-changing morning. For one, the tide was high enough for everyone to paddle over the shallowest part of the reef. An hour's difference and Holt would have been forced to carry Bethany over the jagged reef or paddle the long way around the wide-open bay, which would have taken much longer.

The amount of bleeding for the trauma of the wound wasn't nearly as severe as it could have been. After all, the shark's ragged teeth had severed a major artery. Dr. Ken Pierce, the emergency room doctor that day and a fellow surfer, was waiting when Bethany came in. Dr. Pierce had treated Noah's friend Mike Coots, who experienced a shark-inflicted amputation a few years earlier, in 1998. He explained to us that sometimes when there is such a severe wound the damaged veins actually curl up, especially in muscles that are strong and healthy, helping to restrict the loss of blood. And we can never forget or repay Holt's and Byron's coolheaded actions. Regardless of any personal fear or shock Holt was feeling on the inside, it was his quick thinking and controlled actions that saved Bethany's life, for which I will be forever grateful.

Then there were the comforting words the paramedic, with whom we had attended church, whispered into Bethany's ear as she was loaded into the ambulance: "God will never leave you nor forsake you," he said. These words set the stage for what was to come.

As for me, I was frantic after hearing the news, rushing off to the hospital without my son, who was as worried over his sister as I was. I wanted to hear from Bethany what she thought following the shark attack, as the Blanchards worked to save her life. She kind of blushed when I asked her and said, "Well, the first thing that came to mind was, *Will I lose my sponsors?*"

Nobody really knows how he or she will react in a major crisis, or in surfing terms, "the impact zone," until you are in the thick of it.

When I was speeding to the hospital down the two-lane country highway, I wasn't thinking any of these things, nor did I know anything that had happened on the beach. All I knew was that a shark had attacked Bethany.

Then my cell phone rang. It was Holt.

"Where are you?"

"Driving to the hospital." My voice sounded hollow.

"That's good," he said softly

"How is she? What happened?"

"You . . . you don't know?" He paused. "Cheri . . . her arm is gone."

In my mind, I had imagined a mangled wound that would require loads of stitches and months of rehab; but at that point, I lost it. I dropped the phone and pulled over to the side of the road, unable to drive because of my tears. Then I heard sirens, and soon an ambulance roared past me. I knew most likely that Bethany was in it. I managed to get a grip on my crying and sped after it.

In my fraught state of mind, I remembered that in times of trouble it was a good thing, according to the psalms, to worship God. Bethany and I had been playing a David Crowder CD, so I turned it up super loud and sang along in worship to God through a curtain of tears.

I got about five miles down the road before I saw blue lights and heard a siren behind me.

"Going pretty fast," said the officer after I pulled over.

How does one explain the situation? I tried, and I'm afraid the words were coming out all jumbled. But the reports of the attack were already all over the island, including on all the police radios, so he warned me not to race the ambulance, that I needed to get there safely, not as a car wreck victim, and then he let me go. There could have been three of us in the operating room!

As I was chasing the ambulance and being pulled over, Noah was catching a ride to the hospital with Sarah Hill. He made phone calls on the way, desperate for information, but so few people had anything more than scraps of news.

Mike Dennis, an avid surfer and family friend who lives near Tunnels, was home when Noah called. Knowing that he lived close to Tunnels, Noah asked him to try to scout out the situation. Mike, also a waiter at Tom's workplace, didn't know anything but had heard the ambulance fly by only minutes earlier. He promised he would ride his bike immediately over to the tiny parking lot at Tunnels and scout out the situation. It wasn't long before Mike gave Noah the dire news.

In the uncomfortable tension of the unknown, Sarah said she'd been praying nonstop since she'd first heard that something had happened to Bethany. Specifically, she'd prayed that

God would inspire her with a passage of Scripture to comfort our family. "Jeremiah 29:11," she said to Noah in the tense silence as they drew close to the hospital: " 'For I know the plans I have for you,' declares the LORD, 'plans to prosper you and not to harm you, plans to give you hope and a future' " (*NIV*).

This verse has become the cornerstone of hope for all that we have been through and may go through still. I don't know how deeply those words penetrated Noah on that alarming day in the car ride to the hospital, but in the weeks ahead, they would provide encouragement to all of us and even more so in years to come.

Noah's cell phone rang. It was Mike Dennis calling back. Bethany had lost her whole arm.

Noah managed a thank-you and hung up. While his stomach twisted into knots, he leaned out Sarah's car window, feeling close to throwing up.

Tim was in Kapaa High School when he got the news, or at least a garbled version of it. The message was about a family member being in the hospital, which of course was information he already knew, since he had dropped his father off for knee surgery. But then a second phone call clarified what had really happened earlier that morning, and he bolted from study hall without a word, racing his four-speed Suzuki to the hospital.

Speaking of Tom, although he was already at the hospital, he probably had the worst time of all of us when it came to finding out about Bethany's attack. Tom had already received the anesthetic for his knee surgery and was numb from the waist down. They were about to cut into him in the operating room when news came of a shark attack victim being transported for immediate emergency surgery.

Dr. David Rovinsky, the orthopedic surgeon, and a surfer as well, came in and told Tom that his surgery would have to be postponed as the operating room was needed for a shark attack victim—a 13-year-old girl.

Tom turned ashen; he knew there were only two 13-year-old girls who would be surfing on a school day. "Who is it?" asked Tom.

"I don't know. I'll go find out," said Dr. Rovinsky. He left but soon came back with the fateful news: "A young female from the North Shore."

Dr. Rovinsky saw the look on my husband's face. "Tom, I'll go and find out what I can."

For Tom, it had to be the longest five minutes of his life as he waited for Dr. Rovinsky to return.

When he did, his face was colorless. "Tom, it's Bethany." His voice was soft. "They say she is stable, but that's all I know. But I do need to take you out of here; we are going to need this room for Bethany."

While family and friends began to arrive at the hospital, Tom lay alone on his gurney, helplessly trying to will his numb and useless legs to walk.

Bethany was about to go into the operating room when I arrived. I was ushered into a large conference room where early arrivals were gathering. I not only found Noah, Timmy and Sarah, but also many friends and neighbors—at least 30 people. And more were coming, as it was still early.

Soon, the hospital administrator came to take me to see Bethany.

I thought my heart would leap out of my chest. She was awake and gave me a soft smile.

She's alive! Thank You, Lord, she is alive! I rejoiced.

I just looked at her with tears in my eyes, and I noticed a red leash draped across her stomach. I recognized it as Holt's and went to slip it off to return it to him, when I was stopped by one of the doctors.

"Leave it!" he said. "It is still serving as a tourniquet, and we don't want to remove it until we are in the operating room."

I looked into her eyes and down at her sandy feet and said, "It's going to be okay." Then we both laughed a little because she knew that I disliked that line. I had always pointed out that in movies someone always says it is going to be okay even after the most devastating blow, and life will never be the same. Just like Helen says it in *Soul Surfer*. It's the line people say when something terrible happens and a character steps up to the victim who has just lost her husband in a plane crash or received a letter saying her eldest son has been killed in battle.

It makes me absolutely crazy, and Bethany knows it. It's become a kind of private joke between us. I even go so far as to shout at the TV, "What do you mean, it's going to be all right? How can it ever be all right? This person just lost a loved one and their whole world has changed, *how is it going to be all right?!*"

Maybe the trigger for my excessive reaction is that it was the same comment my aunt said to me when my parents said they were going to divorce. It wasn't all right, and it never was all right with me. Their divorce was *always* a painful thing.

But when I said those words to Bethany, lying there with a surfboard leash keeping her from bleeding to death (she had lost almost 60 percent of her blood) . . . I just *knew* it was going to be all right. I wasn't claiming there wouldn't be struggles or complications on the road ahead; I just sensed that with God's help, everything was going to be all right according to His will. I knew as I said it that Bethany would grasp both our private joke and the fact that, in this case, I was being utterly honest.

My husband was not forgotten for too long. As soon as I had seen Bethany, I found Tom and assured him that she was in good hands. We both shed some tears and prayed together as he waited for feeling to return to his legs.

Meanwhile, Bethany was undergoing surgery. Dr. Rovinsky and his team were taking great care to make sure the wound was completely clean before sewing it up, as shark bites are prone to certain types of bacterial infections.

The hospital conference room continued to fill up with friends, neighbors and fellow believers from all over the island. The "coconut wireless" was in full force along with the outpouring of prayers, which helped pave the way for the amazing things that were to follow in the wake of our tragedy.

But I was not in mourning. I was actually filled with joy and thanksgiving that Bethany was safe and alive, even if she was not completely whole. The shock and fear of the morning's anxiety had been replaced by an exhausted peace.

My mom, who was living on the east side of Kauai at the time, arrived just in time for the hospital nurse to take us up to Bethany's room to wait for her arrival from surgery. When Bethany finally came out, I followed the gurney into her room and sank onto the chair beside her. Grandma was there too, and it wasn't long before we all tenderly laughed together when Bethany threw up her Raisin Bran breakfast!

Family members and close friends began to slip in and out. The room started to fill with flowers, cards and balloons—so many that we even filled the shower stall with them. I remember thinking that the clinical hospital room had been transformed into something like the Garden of Eden by all the beautiful and fragrant bouquets.

At last Tom made it to Bethany's bedside, having finally gained the use of his legs. The doctors said that because our daughter had lost so much blood, transfusions would be necessary. Under the circumstances, we cautiously agreed and gave our permission.

For some reason, this fact sparked Tom to react strongly. He demanded to know whether the hospital was sure their blood supply was safe. It was unsettling to see how Tom wrestled with his strained emotions. He certainly was not reacting to the situation the way I was. For him, seeing his little girl hurt, and having no one to blame or no way to fix it, hit him hard.

In situations like this, people tend to blame God. *Why her?* My husband was about to begin a long and arduous struggle with questioning God's goodness. He kept it to himself, but the thought was there, mulling over inside of him for a long time.

That is the thing: Who deserves tragedy or any circumstance, good or bad? Aren't we all just sinners saved by grace? Waters rise and storms rage; life is full of unavoidable crises. Only God can still the raging storm and keep us in the palm of His hand.

Tom didn't have much time to analyze his anguish and despair. There was a hospital full of caring friends who just wanted to put their arms around him and our family and let him know how much they cared.

Little did we know that there was a full-on media circus heading to Kauai to get the scoop on this gripping story that would unfurl on news channels for days: a young up-and-coming teen surfer mauled by a shark . . . who lives to tell about it. But the wave of head-spinning insanity hadn't yet descended on us, and at that moment, in that hospital room, breathing in the sweet aroma of arriving flowers and staring at the huge bandage covering the empty space where Bethany's left arm should have been, all I could say was, *Thank You, God, for saving her life.*

Our journey to this place had begun long ago; but from this moment on, it was about to go down a wildly different path than any of us could have ever foreseen, and bring us hope in the darkness.

The Shark with a Ragged Fin

*Can you pull in the leviathan with a fishhook or
tie down his tongue with a rope? Can you put a cord through
his nose or pierce his jaw with a hook?*

JOB 41:1-2

He has made me his target.

JOB 16:12

The sun was setting when our week spent in the hospital ended. Tom and I were finalizing our exit when Billy Hamilton, Tom's former roommate, came to the hospital room to give his aloha to Bethany. Billy is considered one of the most well-known and influential surfers in the world. He approached Tom and said in a quiet tone, "I think the shark that attacked Bethany is the same one that has been spotted roaming around the North Shore surf breaks. This shark went after a few other surfers in several different locations. It is acting vicious and appears to be a rogue shark. It won't be long before it will hurt someone else."

"How can you be sure it's the same one, Bill?"

"It has a really distinctive ragged fin," Bill replied. "It swam right through the lineup in Hanalei, harassed a diver and surfers." His voice was firm. "And, Tom, the lifeguards at Tunnels were searching for the shark on their jet skis along with a big cooler of ice in case they found her arm. They said they saw the shark, with its ragged fin, just after the attack. The beast had dry-docked itself upon the reef and then wriggled off. Tom, I think there's something seriously wrong with that animal. Would you be okay if we hunted it down?"

Tom knew that Bill Hamilton wasn't over-reacting. Bill was an accomplished waterman, fisherman, surfboard maker and pioneering surf legend the world over. Bill is father to the world-renowned big-wave surfer Laird Hamilton and his brother, Lyon. Laird actually introduced his mother to Bill, and they ended up marrying soon after. Laird noticed Bill while watching him surf in the waves on the North Shore of Oahu.

In the movies, sharks are often portrayed as attacking everything and anything, particularly humans. In reality, sharks are just predatory fish that usually do not go out of their way to attack people when there is such an abundance of their natural prey. Animals will sometimes attack when threatened, but a shark that consistently goes after surfers isn't feeling threatened; it's moved beyond being a normal predator to a rogue.

To anyone not from a beach culture and, in particular, to anyone not from Hawaii, it might seem like a non-issue to hunt down a shark that was going after people at popular surf or swimming areas. But every surfer knows that encountering sharks is an inherent risk to the sport. A rogue shark, however, is a little different. This big fish is going out of its way to harass humans.

There was another possible objection. In Hawaii, there are those who have kept the embers of the ancient Hawaiian culture alive. The shark, or *mano*, was an *aumakua*, or family god, to be protected from harm. In ancient times it was believed that a departed family member would turn into a shark or that a departed spirit would possess a shark. Often a particular shark was believed to be a specific dead relative, and the creature might even be fed and cared for by the family. Although many Hawaiians do not hold to these old animist beliefs, there has been a resurgence of these ideas among some groups.

Tom weighed these considerations before replying. Then he said, "You would make my day . . . in fact, you would make my *year* if you were able to get that monster. I never want another family to go through what we're going through."

After talking about it together, Tom, Bill and I agreed that if we did go after it, we would have to do it right. Bill teamed up with another local legend for the shark hunt. He was a leathery skinned, white-bearded sea dog and professional fisherman named Ralph Young. Ralph, for many decades, was one of the best longboarders on Kauai. In the local annual Pine Trees surf competitions, Ralph and Billy were usually neck and neck for first place wins.

In Hawaii, it is important to show respect; the community is too small and tightly knit to ride roughshod without considering others. They talked to key members of the Hawaiian community, many of them surfers themselves. After hearing the evidence for a rogue shark with a distinct ragged fin, the majority gave their thumbs-up.

The hunt was on for the ragged-finned shark!

From the many sightings and the size of the shark bite in Bethany's surfboard, Bill Hamilton and Ralph Young estimated the shark to be 12 to15 feet long. Catching it wouldn't be easy.

Ralph knew of an underwater spring near a popular surf break where the shark had been frequently sighted. According to him, the place seemed to attract sharks that were spawning their young—something that happened near that time of year.

Bill and Ralph decided they would set the bait at night because attracting sharks in the day could endanger those surfing nearby. They used a steel cable, anchoring their bait on a large hook connected to a buoy. A 15-foot tiger shark can weigh close to 2,000 pounds, and its jaws have enough force to snap anything less substantial. At first light, the two fishermen returned to see if anything had paid a visit overnight. At the break of dawn Ralph found the bait half gone.

The following morning the bait was gone, and to their astonishment the hook was completely straight! Something big was lurking around the spring.

"Well," said Ralph when he saw the undoing, "I've got to get a little more serious."

The next night, they used a massive hook that Ralph had brought home from New Zealand for hunting this kind of huge animal. As bait they used a Galapagos shark, one of the most abundant species of sharks in island waters. Over the next few days they baited huge hooks and anchored them deep in the bay.

On the fifth day, Ralph went out to check and saw that the lines and buoys had become tangled. He put on a dive mask and leaned over the boat. There on the bottom, firmly caught on the cable, was a massive Tiger shark with a distinctive ragged dorsal fin.

The two men hoisted up the shark and towed it to the beach where a backhoe was enlisted to get the shark out of the water. The 14-and-a-half-foot shark began to attract a crowd on the beach, and Ralph and Bill didn't want to cause a scene. They used their two small boats to haul the shark out to sea so they could cut the stomach open to examine the contents.

The stomach was empty.

Ralph had seen this before. As he explained to us later, sharks (particularly Tiger sharks) will fill their bellies with so much inedible garbage, including rocks, cans and trash, that they will actually turn their stomachs inside out to regurgitate the contents. And, if he were correct, the large chunk of surfboard made of fiberglass and foam, which the shark had eaten (along with our daughter's arm and her wristwatch), would cause the shark to disgorge its stomach. Not just because it was inedible, he said, but also because it could have seriously disrupted the shark's buoyancy.

It was the ragged fin that told them they'd gotten the shark that had been hunting surfers. It correlated to the many other eyewitness accounts, including that of the Tunnels' lifeguards. But was it for sure the one that attacked Bethany?

Ralph and Bill carefully took the tender stomach skin to give to a Hawaiian drum maker and then loaded the giant carcass with rocks and sent it back into the ocean, but not before cutting out the huge jaw. There was one last test before knowing for sure whether the hunt had been a success.

Tom and Bethany took her mutilated surfboard down to Ralph's *hale*. They carefully matched the gaping jaws with the shape of the crescent torn out of the red, white and blue board. It was a perfect match! They had found the rogue shark.

While we certainly don't celebrate the destruction of one of God's creatures, I have to admit that it made all of us feel very good to know this particular animal would not be preying on any other surfers, divers or swimmers. Tom, in particular, was extremely thankful that through the determined efforts of his friends Ralph and Bill, the shark that had caused us such grief would not go on to cause an even greater tragedy for another family.

Months later, Ralph gave each member of the family a tooth from the jaws. To Tom's surprise, Bethany tentatively smiled as she received hers. This ceremonial gesture brought closure to this traumatic chapter in our lives.

Fearless Passion

*No eye has seen, no ear has heard, no mind has conceived
what God has prepared for those who love him.*

1 CORINTHIANS 2:8-10, *NIV*

*Cast your cares on the LORD and He will sustain you;
He will never let the righteous be shaken.*

PSALM 55:22, *TNIV*

We spent five nights in the hospital.

Our emotions continued to be raw and would sometimes burst through the dam of self-control, stunning us. Tom was numb with a sense of disbelief that he couldn't shake, but I believed that we were completely in God's hands.

Tom recalls that when he drove home to get us all some fresh clothes and check on Hana, our dog, he melted down in tears, pulling over to the side of the road until he could compose himself. I told Tom about the conversation and prayer Bethany and I had shared when we asked God to use her surfing for His glory. I told him how we had asked God to let her be a light for Him in the world of surfing. The apparent unreasonableness of God to take away his daughter's dreams needled Tom, and anger quietly simmered inside of him.

Holt, too, was struggling. He blamed himself for what happened, even though we saw him as the hero who saved our daughter's life. He felt that he should not have encouraged the girls to go surfing that day. The waves had been small, not even worth it. He kept going over why he hadn't just said never mind and driven them all safely home.

Tom found himself encouraging Holt over and over that he shouldn't feel responsible in any way for the attack. Every surfer knows there is a risk of sharks, improbable though it is; but the passion for surfing outweighs common sense and they still choose to paddle out. He told Holt how much we all appreciated what he had done to save Bethany—without him she would have died.

The memory of that Halloween morning kept rising up in Holt's mind like an incoming tide. At the same time, Holt was trying to bolster Tom's warring emotions with hope-filled words. He knew how much Bethany's surfing successes meant to her and to all of us. While Bethany was still in the hospital, Holt would describe possible scenarios for her continuing surf career, "She could probably still compete as a long boarder."

Our internal and emotional struggles were not the only things with which we were wrestling. News of the shark attack spread like wildfire through the coconut wireless alongside the growing media as news outlets picked up on the story and sent their reporters to Kauai. I had stayed in the hospital room with Bethany to manage the flow of visiting friends and well-wishers, but Tom found himself having to juggle a growing crowd and camera crews in the lobby. The reporters' endless questions were wearing on him. He couldn't turn them away, but his mind and heart were with Bethany.

One of Tom's old surf buddies from Oahu, Steve Cranston, jumped in to put a buffer between our family and the press, helping to make some sense out of the chaos. With his help, we picked one reporter, Guy Hagi, a newscaster and surfer from Oahu, to give an exclusive television interview. Steve and the hospital staff, especially Lani Yukimura, went to great lengths to insulate us from the growing chaos as everyone, it seemed, was trying to get an interview with Bethany.

Sarah Hill, more than anyone else outside the family, was present during those long days at Wilcox Hospital. Sarah took a week off from work, arriving in the morning and staying until late at night. Shortly after Bethany came out of surgery, Sarah was on hand. Thirteen-year-old Bethany's words struck her: "Sarah, I just prayed and prayed the whole way to the beach. I'm glad this happened to me and not to Alana. I don't know if her faith is ready to handle this kind of thing." Sarah marveled at Bethany's heart and resilience, and it was with Sarah that Bethany first brought up the possibility of a return to surfing.

In a quiet, intimate moment when visitors and family weren't crowding the room, Bethany said to Sarah in a voice of resignation, "Maybe I could be a professional soccer player or photographer, or something."

Sarah encouraged her, "If you ask me, God gave you the *gift* of surfing, and I don't think He has taken it away from you."

I will admit that none of us were as bold or reckless in our imagination as that. We were confident that Bethany would at least be able to enjoy swimming. Tim even bought her a pair of fins with the suggestion that she could now join him catching waves on a body board; but as for her dream of being a professional surfer, it seemed to be shattered.

But Sarah didn't give up! She ministered hope to us as well and shared the Jeremiah 29:11 passage that God had brought to her mind as she raced to the hospital with Noah. Hearing those words, hearing her fervent trust in what God could do, we became aware that God Himself had stepped into the midst of a tragic situation and flooded it with hope and promise.

Meanwhile, in the hospital room overflowing with flowers and stuffed animals, Bethany was quickly healing, getting stronger and starting to become restless. More and more, Bethany's indomitable spirit led her to find an excuse to get out of bed. One day she grabbed a couple of balloons and took them out to the hallway to bat them around like any rambunctious, slightly bored kid might do. She was smiling and having a grand old time, never mind that her left arm had been mauled off days before. I saw the look on her face; and at that moment, I could see hope.

The visitors continued to stream in. Next came the whole lifeguard crew from the North Shore. On Sunday, the youth pastor brought church to Bethany in the form of the youth group and some guitars, and there were plenty of visitors from the other churches—pastors, elders and kids. Mike Coots, who I mentioned before as having lost his leg in a shark attack in 1998, was particularly helpful, as he understood exactly what Bethany was going through.

By the end of our time in the hospital, we were ready to go home.

We needed some quiet time to heal. Thankfully, some friends managed to find us a secluded beach home outside a little town called Anahola, and we escaped the hospital by the back door. Bethany jumped in Sarah's car because it had tinted windows and was not as recognizable as our blue beast of a van.

The beach house turned out to be a wonderful gift.

The home had enough bedrooms for each of us, a hot tub and, best of all, the ocean right outside the back door. Only a few people knew where we were, so we could spend time sorting out our emotions privately. To be honest, Tom and I often took turns crying alone in our room that week.

Near the end of our stay, the late Andy Irons stopped by. Andy was a North Shore boy whose surfing ability had flung him into a battle for the world championship. We'd known him since he was a kid and watched him and his brother Bruce grow up into surf champions. He'd known the girls, too, though they were much younger and somewhat mischievous (because he lived near Alana, the girls would sometimes play doorbell ditch at his house).

Andy was on his way to surf the Pipe Masters on Oahu, but he brought a huge teddy bear with him.

"I wish I could stay longer," he told Bethany, choking up when he saw her bandaged arm, "but the contest is tomorrow."

"Win it for me," she said to him.

And he did.

While we stayed at that beach house, our family attempted to decompress the recent events that had bowled us over. We talked a lot, hung out in the hot tub, read, prayed and walked along the beach. Tim brought down a stack of body boarding videos for us, knowing that Bethany might not want to watch stand-up surfing just yet, the loss of her dream so fresh.

But there were times when we got bored with just hanging around the house. We were active people. We needed adventure, or something!

One day, Bethany, Alana and Sarah decided to go to the local market to rent a video. They thought it would be fun to disguise Bethany in a wig, a hat and sunglasses so she wouldn't be recognized. Tim even made her an arm out of paper towel rolls and stuffed her into a long-sleeved shirt.

It worked! No one recognized them until they were on their way out of the store and they passed surfing legend Titus Kinimaka. He looked at her strange getup and just said, "Hey, Bethany."

Our time at this house was an emotional watershed for our whole family, but we had more things than just our inner hearts to consider. Would Bethany need a prosthetic arm? Rehabilitation? The weight of imagined bills pressed on us.

Prosthetics had come a long way in assisting an amputee to have a semblance of normalcy. But some suggestions were just counterproductive, such as a treatment to extend the bone remnant and then attach rods and electronics to interface with a robotic arm. Water combined with electricity? If Bethany were ever going to get back in the ocean, anything electronic would be useless. The dollar amounts tossed around for even the simplest of prosthetic devices could be staggering.

But the incredible people in our tight-knit community began doing amazing things to bless us. *Amazing* things. Within two weeks, a group of friends, spearheaded by Jill Smith and Amy Marvin, had managed to organize a grassroots nonprofit organization—the Friends of Bethany Hamilton—that exists to this day. Its primary focus is to support shark attack survivors and amputees worldwide and present inspiring life stories through movies, projects and activities.

A massive fund-raiser was held at the Marriot Hotel. Friends donated surfboards, artwork, crafts and more for a silent auction to help Bethany. Tom and the boys attended, but Bethany was not ready for the exposure, so I stayed home with her.

We didn't quite expect the overflowing generosity, love and support from everyone all over the island. As the second week drew to a close, we realized that awareness of our story had grown much larger than just our island, or even our state.

Suddenly, we were dealing with stacks of mail and gifts that arrived for Bethany. In 24 hours, before the advent of Twitter and Facebook, she got 7,000 emails wishing her a speedy recovery and cheering her on. The kindness and comfort of total strangers was overwhelming to us. But in a way, they weren't strangers; something in Bethany's experience had resonated with them and had connected them to her. Something that really touched us was that many of the cards and letters were from kids.

There was no humanly possible way to respond to each and every one of the cards, letters and emails, but Bethany, Alana, Sarah and I would try to read each one, setting aside any that we felt needed an answer.

Eventually, our time at the beach house drew to a close. We were ready to go home after all the dramatic events of the previous two weeks. Once we settled back into the familiar, Bethany was anxious to get back in the water; but because she still had stitches, it was against doctor's orders.

The movie portrayed me as going with Bethany to the hospital, but it was actually Tom. On the day she was scheduled to have her stitches out, Tom, who had finally had his knee surgery, was also to have his stitches removed. The two of them returned to Dr. Rovinsky together. Tom's few stitches were quick and painless to remove. Bethany's were a different matter. Her sutures were deep, and there were lots of them.

As the doctor began removing each stitch, Tom noticed that Bethany's face was pale. But by the time they were ready to leave the doctor's office, Bethany had composed herself and even got a little of her buoyant nature back. She turned to Dr. Rovinsky and said, "So, can I go in the ocean now?"

Rovinsky waved a warning finger. "No, no!" he replied, and then, pointing to the little holes left by the stitches, said, "You see these little *pukas*? They have to be closed or bacteria from the ocean or streams could get in there, and then you would really have trouble."

It seemed at this moment that the actuality of what had happened to her and what it would mean finally struck her. She began to cry deep, sobbing tears, and Tom wept with her.

As the tears subsided, Dr. Rovinsky, himself a surfer, said with a wink, "It should be healed enough by Thanksgiving Day."

Bethany looked up at him and smiled, "Thanksgiving Day?"

She had been given a target date for normal life to begin again.

Life in the Hamilton household was anything but back to normal. Or, I should say, we were forced to make some adjustments around the "new" normal.

We soon encountered unforeseen things that were challenging for someone with one arm, but Bethany was already showing that remarkable ability to adapt that has amazed so many people. I replaced her closet coat hangers with hooks—lots and lots of hooks—to hang her clothes on. At the hospital, a therapist taught Bethany to tie her shoes with one hand, but we found it easier to just tie them loosely enough for her to slip on. Bethany seldom wore anything but sandals or the typical "rubba slippahs" popular across Hawaii.

I tried to do things to make it easier for her to navigate around the house. I bought chairs for our dining room table that were lightweight and easy to move, and I bought funnels to help her pour water or her almond milk. There were so many things you take for granted, so many tasks you do without thinking about. Just pouring liquid becomes a trial when you can't steady the cup with the other hand. Sometimes it was hard for me to watch, but I focused on the question, "What can I do to help her?"

Trial and error was our new way of life. Things that had taken mere seconds to accomplish now took minutes. And how do you gracefully put toothpaste on the brush with one hand?

Then there were the things that Bethany would no longer get to use or enjoy. She had been learning to play worship songs on the guitar. I took the guitar out of her room with a strange feeling in my heart. I set it next to my keyboard and wondered if she might like piano lessons instead.

As Thanksgiving Day drew nearer, the question of Bethany surfing again cropped up. And Bethany's youth group started showing up again. The day before Thanksgiving, the trade winds switched. A westerly wind combined with a rising swell that set off a few lesser-known surf spots.

The phone rang. It was for Bethany. The beach break called Rock Quarry was as good as it gets, did she want to come?

You should have seen the way her eyes glowed at the news.

Noah in particular knew what it meant. The lure of great waves was working on his sister. He knew how badly she wanted to try surfing again. Noah had worked hard on an agreement with the television show *Inside Edition* that if Bethany ever tried to go out and surf again, he'd get them an interview and exclusive video in exchange for a prosthetic arm for her.

Noah was adamant. If Bethany went to the beach with her friends, she was NOT to surf.

The beach was packed with North Shore surfers, the Irons brothers, Holt, Alana, Sarah and all the rest of the Hanalei surf team. Sitting on the beach, just watching the perfect surf peel across the sand, was too much for Bethany. Excitement burned in her heart. Sarah saw it, and so did Holt.

"You can use one of my boards," he said.

Bethany turned to Sarah. "I'm going to pretend that you tried to stop me."

"Wait, I'm going with you!" said Sarah.

Officially, "nothing" happened. But I can tell you that Bethany went up and down the beach, begging everyone not to take a picture of her; otherwise, she might not get her prosthetic arm. Not one person lifted a camera, but people on the beach were crying. Tim and Noah got there just in time to film her first ride.

The next day, Thanksgiving, with intense anticipation, I watched as Bethany went out surfing for the first time. Tom brought her my long board to use, which was heavier and more stable than a regular short board. As she waxed up her board and wrestled with the leash, Tom offered to push her into the waves like he had when she was little, but Bethany rebuffed him.

"No, Dad, I have to do it myself."

Her initial attempts at catching a wave were painful to watch. Our hearts felt heavy as lead. Catching waves with one arm is difficult; but pushing off a board that's sliding down a wave as you try to stand up is much more so. The few times Bethany was able to get to her feet showed how much she'd have to relearn about balance with one arm missing. Bethany, who had been such a strong surfer just a few weeks before, struggled and flailed like a beginner.

"Put your hand in the center of the board," Tom shouted over the noise of the surf. "You won't dig the rail into the water that way."

Bethany paddled back out, tenaciously trying again and again. All of a sudden, something seemed to click. She got up and found the balance point. Her naturally fluid style came back, and she surfed the wave all the way to the beach.

The beach erupted with cheers, and every surfer in the lineup started hooting and calling out with excitement. Pros and tourists alike were caught up in the moment. Tom went wild, barely able to contain the joy that coursed through him. Noah and Timmy were whooping and screaming. And, of course, the cameras clicked and the video cameras rolled.

I joined in the elation. I was thrilled at what my daughter had accomplished, and I knew it wouldn't be long before she would be back out having fun with her friends. But I couldn't see competition in her future.

Tom made it his mission to help Bethany progress back to where she had been before the attack. Every morning, he and Bethany would get up and go to Pine Trees or Waikokos so that she could relearn the cadence of paddling, catching a wave, getting to her feet and balancing with one arm.

She advanced, but the slow progress was discouraging for Tom. One day, as Tom retells it, he was sitting under the palms at Pine Trees, having his own little pity party and grumbling at God because He'd allowed this to happen to Bethany. He was tired of watching her struggle to push through the surf while holding onto the board with one hand.

On that particular day, there was a riptide running hard, and one of the many tourists had accidentally gotten herself stuck in it. The lifeguards had already spotted her, and Tom watched as they quickly paddled out to the woman on a huge yellow rescue board with handles built onto it. The woman grabbed hold of a handle as the lifeguards effortlessly pulled her back to the beach.

Tom says it was almost like a cartoon when the light bulb appears over the character's head.

"A handle! A handle in the middle of the board!"

Tom fished from his pocket a small black notebook he always carried with him and sketched the outline of a surfboard. Dead center, under the nose, he drew a handle. It was as if God had stripped away Tom's gloominess just to show him how trivial such problems are.

A custom board was made for Bethany. It had a handle exactly where Tom had sketched it.

And it worked.

Now Bethany could use one hand to dive deep under oncoming waves and get quickly out into the lineup.

As her performance and confidence increased, Tom kept patiently encouraging her. He knew that Bethany was determined to compete. I, on the other hand, while overjoyed at her progress, couldn't envision that possibility in her future. But maybe, said a secret part of my heart, just maybe . . .

Another change was taking place in the weeks after the shark attack. It was a change within Tom. Only he can tell you the exact time and place it happened, but what I do know was that Tom had been a spiritual bump on a log. He was defeated, immersed in self-pity, just going through the motions.

The breakthrough happened while at church. We had not stopped going, but one day, as we were singing a worship song, Tom realized that he was not singing, nor had he been singing at all since the attack.

Tom loves to sing. He has a great voice, and worshiping God with music is one of the key ways the Lord touches him, but he couldn't find his voice. It had been stilled amid all the dark-winged confusion, hurt, anger and pain. Every single time that he'd asked, "Why her, God?" insurmountable pain assailed him. He was standing in an attitude of worship, but he was not worshiping.

Then God impressed upon his heart, "You're going to worship Me in heaven some day so you need to worship Me on earth."

At that moment, Tom realized that every second he'd been busy blaming God was a second he'd not been able to be truly thankful that we still had Bethany with us. He thanked God then, praised Him for the gift of Bethany's life—and more than that, God impressed on his heart that He had greater things in store for our family, and for Bethany, than we could ever realize.

And then he sang.

When Tom had his big breakthrough, I was still struggling with my own. You see, while I believed in Bethany, I also was afraid that I'd see her fail. I wanted her to reach for all of her dreams, but I thought Tom was pushing her too hard and too fast. She'd been at the top, but that was then. I feared she'd be devastated by her disappointment. I feared her failure.

The National Scholastic Surfing Association (NSSA) regional surfing event was scheduled to take place in January 2004, on the Big Island of Hawaii. Bethany had been back in the water since Thanksgiving. It was barely three months since she had lost her arm in the shark attack; but she decided to enter the contest.

She told her dad before she told me. I would have told her it was too soon to compete. Tom, well, he apparently saw the fire in her eyes and thought she had a shot at it. Or more accurately, he thought she deserved a shot at it.

Everyone went to the Big Island but me. I couldn't watch her fail; it would be more than I could take. Even staying home, I was very nervous for her. Surf contests are highly competitive events. The best surfers in the world are trying to outmaneuver and outsurf every other contestant. Boys' or girls' division, it didn't matter, surf contests were seriously tough.

Tom and I had talked about the risks. If she totally failed, she would be demoralized or crushed. We talked about everything that might go wrong, but if you know Bethany, you know that she won't quit, and she won't deliver less than 100 percent.

Tom had to tell me how it went when they got back. No one but the director of the contest had known that she had entered, so when Bethany showed up on the sand in her contest jersey, everyone's jaws dropped.

She didn't catch as many waves as the other competitors in her heat, but the ones she did catch she tore up. She placed fifth in her entire age division, a big deal for any female surfer—but a massive achievement for a young woman who had just lost her arm.

The families who had brought their kids out to surf in the competition all clustered around Bethany when she came out of the water, their faces reflecting the radiant triumph on her face. Tom stood on the beach off to one side, joy and pride in his daughter filling him with an even deeper satisfaction now that he'd made peace with God.

That was when the legendary wave rider and professional surfing coach Ben Aipa walked up to him and said softly, "I tried to video Bethany's first wave, but I was so overcome with emotion that I had to put the camera down. She's got the will and the heart and desire to take this as far as she wants to go. I would consider it an honor if I could be her coach."

Bethany was back.

The following year, she would not just place in the NSSA National Contest, she would win the Explorer Women's Division!

A Surfer Girl Who Loves God

You will be a crown of splendor in the Lord's hand,
a royal diadem in the hand of your God.

ISAIAH 62:3

It soon became clear that we had been in the calm center of a different sort of hurricane. When Bethany paddled out into that NSSA competition, charging hard just a few weeks after the attack, the calm eye of the storm was moving, and we were now at an epicenter, sensing something way bigger than us. We were at the point where we could just open up the floodgates without holding back and try to ride the media tidal wave. But you don't ride tidal waves; they swamp you.

When we sat down with Sarah Hill, it took our family only a few minutes to define our central criterion for granting interview requests: Our family's purpose was to lift up the name of Christ. We needed someone who could help us take advantage of all the interest while being committed to our boundaries and beliefs—someone who would help manage Bethany while never, ever compromising our explicit purpose and mission.

Before the attack, Tom had been in contact with an entrepreneur named Roy Hofstetter about possibly promoting Bethany's surfing career. Roy's daughter Chantilly was a classmate of Bethany's, and so Roy was already familiar with her very real surfing talent. Roy's unique experience might help to net a sponsorship deal beyond just the realm of surf culture.

Like almost any other sport, sponsorship is how the athlete really earns his living. Sponsors help defray or fully cover the cost of travel, surfboards and hotel rooms. Our own evaporating money supply would limit how far Bethany could go. Simply put, a good sponsorship deal would enable Bethany to become a serious competitor. We were on the cusp of signing a deal with Roy Hofstetter when Bethany was attacked.

After we saw with our own eyes Bethany's remarkable rebound from calamity and how her story seemed to resonate so powerfully with people across the board, we contacted Roy to see if he would still be willing to help. But now the need was to manage the surge of interest coming our way.

Roy agreed. He would field the requests for interviews, TV and radio appearances and all the other myriad offers we couldn't possibly manage.

This was a tricky decision. We spent a lot of time praying for God's leading and wisdom. We knew that by doing this we might overexpose our daughter. It might be too much, too quick, too soon. So we decided that she had to be 100 percent in agreement with anything we considered. We could always walk away.

I think what kept everything in perspective for us was that we all were committed to using the media attention solely to honor God. Bethany's Christian faith was, and is, central to her character and was what gave her the power to spring back.

Tom and I knew it was just Bethany being herself.

We were able to tell Bethany's story in book form, designed for 14-year-olds and titled *Soul Surfer*, which to our delight found its way into the hands of many young people. We also sought with much more deliberation for the right pace and rhythm that Bethany would be able to handle, and that the rest of us would be able to handle too.

At one point, I was in an SUV rental, crammed tight with surfboards and luggage. Tom, Bethany, Noah and I were going to visit her surfboard shaper in Ventura, California, to pick up a new surfboard he had just finished making. I was feeling lost as we drove through two hours of heavy traffic, wondering what we were doing with our lives. Is this where we wanted to be? Tim was smart to bale on this expedition!

Finally, we reached our destination and took care of business. The shaper gave Bethany her new surfboard with Palm Fronds sprayed green on the surfboard. I looked at the design and was not impressed until I listened to the CD that was given to us, which we played on the two-hour drive back. Palm fronds were used to worship God, waving them up and down to glorify the King of kings and Lord of lords. They were used on the triumphal entry of Jesus into Jerusalem as He declared that He was King. I was overwhelmed at the meaning because this explained what Bethany was called to do. Worship and honor God with her surfing!

When Bethany was invited to throw the opening pitch at a Yankees game in New York City, I didn't go, but Tom was there. Bethany had played a lot of sports, but never baseball, so it fell on Tom to take her to Central Park to work on throwing a baseball 60 feet with some degree of accuracy. He even borrowed a baseball from the nearby Mickey Mantle Restaurant and, using recall from Little League games, worked with Bethany all morning until she could put a ball in the pocket.

Later, at the game, New York Yankees pitcher and fellow believer Randy Johnson told Bethany that his kids had read her book. "Maybe the first time they've read a book from cover to cover," he said with a laugh.

Bethany threw the opening pitch fast and straight, right in the strike zone. The catcher even said it had a little heat on it. All the while, Tom stood in the dugout grinning like the Cheshire Cat and flashing back to the time in his childhood when he stood on that same field with his father as a Little League all star.

My personal favorite was when Bethany threw the opening pitch for the Oakland A's in California. The jumbotrons lit up with video of her surfing to the Beach Boys song "Surfer Girl," and in came Bethany, riding in the back of a red convertible while the U.S. Navy's Blue Angels Squadron streaked overhead with the whole thing finishing with fireworks. Wow!

But it wasn't the events that meant the most to us; it was the people we met who connected to us, who connected with Bethany's story in a meaningful way.

While we were in New York, a guy named Jeff Denholm sought us out. He took the train from his home in Maine in order to be an encouragement to Bethany and us. Jeff had lost most of his arm in an accident on an Alaskan fishing trawler, but he was blessed with a good mind for engineering and the same kind of tenacious spirit as Bethany. Jeff refused to give up surfing, skiing, mountain biking and the other extreme sports he loved. So he had designed a number of ingenious prosthetic attachments for the remnant of his severed arm, ultimately becoming a surfing ambassador for Patagonia Sports. Like Bethany, nothing was going to stop him from living an active lifestyle!

One trip the family took, part business and part pleasure, was unforgettable.

We arrived at Heathrow, in London, a massively huge airport! You could live in this multi-terminal compound and get lost forever! Our family arrived in the United Kingdom with the normal basic jet lag, even though we had seats in which we could lie down and sleep, which saved us. We took a cab to our hotel. This is never an easy feat when traveling with surfboards!

The four of us—Tom, Bethany, Tim and I—were booked into an old classic hotel. Immediately after setting down our luggage in our one room, we all looked for the bathroom. No bathroom! No beds! A nice view, but this wouldn't work out. We called the front desk, and they had us in a side office suite or something. I was happy, because we were moved to an upgrade, which had an amazing view of an old church bell tower that was just begging for my camera.

It was Sunday, so I went down to the concierge to ask if there were any evening church services around that we could go to. He gave me the name of "The American Church" for the "tourists." I said I wanted to go to a church with "locals." He was clueless, so I did my own search in the phone book and found a Calvary Chapel with a six o'clock service.

We took a cab, which was great fun. The English cabs are those old black classic vehicles that smell leathery and look as if they are from the 1940s. I gave the driver the address, and we were dropped off in front of Harry Potter's old school, or a look-alike! It was a quaint old brick school building complete with wrought iron gates. Since we had an hour before the service started, I said, "Let's go take some family pictures at that beautiful old church across the street."

There was a huge courtyard with a few tourists meandering around, but it looked like a service was in progress. We walked over to the entrance of the old church and past some anxious-looking film crew on the opposite courtyard corner. They were so busy looking for their target that we walked right past them with ease. We all laughed because the press was so hungry for

Bethany news, and here she was, but they were too focused to not see her walk right past them.

We walked quietly inside to take a peek and maybe get a few photos, since it was one of the most beautiful churches I had ever seen. It was an ancient building filled with smoke from lit candles; and those from years past had given the ceiling a blackened hue. The architectural design caused you to lift your head and look up toward heaven. There you saw the stained-glass windows telling the gospel stories from God's Word.

The interior design of the building had created one of the best sound features ever. A woman's beautiful voice was singing a cappella, and it cut through the core of my being, making it hard not to cry. I said, "Let's find a seat and listen for a while." The place was packed, but we squeezed into some seats in the back. It turns out we were at a service for the Pope, who had just died on Friday. Tony Blair was there, along with Camilla Parker Bowles, which we read about in the paper the next day. It is nice to do something special without the stress of trying to make it happen. God's timing as our tour guide was impeccable!

When it was almost six o' clock, we made our exit and crossed the street to Harry's school. I had not read the books, as I am not into the occult, but I enjoyed the special effects that this school/movie set had to offer. We gathered in an auditorium with a multicultural crowd that looked like they were from every tribe and nation upon the earth. I relaxed and enjoyed singing with the talented worship team's presentation and lineup of worship songs. Then I broke, and the flood of tears came because they closed the worship with "Blessed Be Your Name," the song that contains the lines from the Old Testament story of Job confessing in worship that God "gives and takes away, blessed be the name of the LORD." God had been ministering to us with that song since day one, our ground zero.

God likes to open up our hard hearts to get His Word inside of our hearts. Sometimes we get so beat up by life that scar tissue hardens and closes us off to His love and ministry. Worship helps to begin healing the damage incurred so that God can bind up our wounds with His love.

The message came next, and I was pleased to listen to the pastor's eloquent English accent. I felt guilty because the sermon was so personal, as if God had prepared a meal just for us. I hope the other people were fed just as much. It is so peaceful to be halfway across the world, and not know anyone except God and experience His love, care and guidance. God could not have planned our day better. Tomorrow we could surf in Cornwall, England!

One other aside: The longest-running kid's show in England is *Blue Peter*. Bethany had been invited to the show to teach the hosts how to surf. The venue for the surf lessons was Fistral Beach on the north coast of Cornwall, where the surf history of England first began. Surf culture is alive and well in Great Britain, contributing to the economy with tourism, fashion and health.

Everyone had decided that the most exciting thing to do with Bethany was learn to surf! They didn't request lessons; they just chose to let you know they were getting lessons! She didn't have it on her résumé, but even so, she is a most excellent teacher. She had more fun watching than anyone, helping everyone wipe out and eat humble pie. The hosts had no problem learning, but they did have the look of natural athletes. Everyone dressed in his finest black wet suit, as it was freezing cold!

I chose to hang out inside the warm beach restaurant with a front-row view and order something hot to drink. On the walls were photos of hot, sunny beach days taken in the warm months of summer, on location with premier-looking waves ridden by surfers in trunks, not wet suits. It does get warm in Cornwall, but only in the late summer months, along with the best swells of the year. So if you're planning any surf expeditions, do your research!

The show aired on European TV, and Bethany was presented with a Blue Peter Badge for courage. The badge provides the wearer with free entry to many British attractions, particularly museums and exhibitions that are featured on the show.

Often, it seems as if Bethany's brothers are just tagging along on her adventures, but I believe that God is directing their lives and using them and preparing them for their futures as He cares for each and every one of us.

Bethany's brother Tim, who was with us on that trip, was filming a video for our family, and he remembered that he had a body-boarding friend who lived in Cornwall. He gave him a call and a visit ensued. Tim's English body-boarding friend and his buddy were planning a trip to Iceland. They invited Tim along and made arrangements with him to hook up for travel after he finished his Bethany tour.

Tim had an amazing, once-in-a-lifetime adventure in Iceland, jumping off icebergs and waterfalls into uncrowded surf! The best part was traveling with adventurous, fun, always laughing guys who make life happen.

Several years after the shark attack, and Bethany's dramatic return to professional surfing, the initial torrent of media attention subsided into a manageable river we had learned to navigate pretty well. There were still some frictions, but overall, we'd only grown stronger and closer together—as well as closer to God.

As Bethany's teen years drew to a close, she got more confident and easy under public scrutiny. Noah and Becky took on the role of managing the business side of things (as well as official photography, video and other artistic elements) so that Bethany could focus on what she does best—surfing.

Our son Tim, mellow and unassuming, spends most of his time filming and editing surf movies. One of his underground films gained quite a cult following among the body board crew.

Sarah Hill has become an integral part of our lives. Bethany, like many teenagers do, had found a mentor to trust in addition to her family.

Bethany had to come to terms with the fact that by being a witness for Christ, there would be plenty of people who would use any excuse to take her down a peg. These were the ones who wouldn't show grace for the fact that she was a normal, fun-loving teenager; or for the fact that our Hawaii-style beach culture didn't always resemble how they thought a good Christian should act or dress. And because she called herself a Christian, people certainly wouldn't let her be anything less than perfect—an unrealistic expectation for anyone.

One thing that deeply impacted Bethany for the good was the time she was able to join the youth group on a mission trip to Tijuana, Mexico. Her brothers had gone a few times in prior years, but Bethany had not yet been able to go. She'd been to Thailand with World Vision in 2005 (our family supports a couple of kids through that organization). There was something special about going as a normal kid on a mission trip with her friends, to help out as best they could.

After hearing some of the crazy stories the boys told of their trips to Mexico, we were a bit concerned about Bethany's safety. But Timmy decided he'd go along as videographer for the entire youth group, and we were relieved.

The youth leaders, including Sarah Hill, took vans full of Kauai kids into the hidden folds of Tijuana, under the watchful eye of Spectrum Ministries based in San Diego (in fact, based out of the same church, Emmanuel, where I'd first attended Vacation Bible School so many years ago!).

There, in the most impoverished of slums, Bethany and her friends washed the lice out of children's hair, distributed blankets and food, set up a mini carnival full of games and prizes, and ran the portable bathhouse, which was the only chance for many of the kids to receive a shower.

For American teenagers, immersion into a world so far removed from their privileged materialism, yet so close—right across the border—was an eye-opening experience. Our kids saw firsthand the power of having a hands-on ministry with the poor and even came back with a story of how Pastor Von, the longtime head of Spectrum Ministries, had his valuables stolen from his car while working the bathhouse only to have them returned the next day by one of Tijuana's feared drug lords, with apologies that the thief was not aware of who he was stealing from. Apparently, the drug lord had been the recipient of the kindness of this ministry in his poverty-stricken childhood, and he never forgot it.

The Mexican kids were very curious about Bethany. Scarcely a single one had heard of her, but naturally they asked her over and over about her missing arm. Bethany quickly figured out the word "shark" in Spanish—*tiburon*. As soon as they heard it, and she pointed to her shoulder, their eyes nearly fell out of their heads. Bethany had their rapt attention as she told her story through a translator.

While there, the group was introduced to a new orphanage that Spectrum had just discovered. The place was in terrible shape, filthy and run-down even for a Mexican orphanage. Many of the kids were sick with a variety of illnesses, and the mothers of several of the children had abandoned them on the streets because they had Down syndrome.

The place had no medicine and little food.

Sarah, Bethany and the kids had already exhausted the cash given to them by the church on other projects. But faced with the dire need of these children, they knew they had to do something. Sarah asked the lady in charge to write a list of absolute needs for the kids. The list was two pages long, and that covered only the bare essentials for the 100 children.

Later that night, Sarah had to admit that there was no practical way to stretch their funds to meet those needs. So she shared the situation with everyone and showed the group the list. And, of course, Bethany grabbed a box and put it on the table. "What about pitching in some of our personal spending money?" she said. Everyone had a few bucks squirreled away for buying something at the Southern California shopping malls they couldn't get in Hawaii (at least without paying through the nose for shipping).

"No one's obligated to put anything in; it'll be totally private. Put in what you want." Bethany pointed to the list, "If you can spare enough for just one of these items, that'll at least be something, right?"

Then they left the box on the table; no one managed it or waited to see who would put in what. When Sarah counted the money the next morning, there was more than $1,500. The group went to Costco in Mexico and filled nine carts full of food, medicine, diapers, soap and cleaning supplies. When they arrived at the orphanage and started unloading everything, the director came out and simply collapsed into Sarah's arms.

Tom and I know that these experiences build something within a person that could never be taught just sitting in church. "Religion that God our Father accepts as pure and faultless is this: to look after orphans and widows in their distress and to keep oneself from being polluted by the world" (Jas. 1:27, *NIV*).

You don't have to have a story like Bethany's to be extraordinary; you just have to be willing for God to have your whole life. God does not guarantee you an easy path—in fact, the road is often difficult. I never would have chosen to have my daughter lose her arm; but when you surrender to God, He sometimes takes away before He gives back.

Bethany has become a symbol of hope and encouragement for many people. That role is not without personal sacrifice.

But there was one more thing that had occasionally cropped up since the attack. For years it had bubbled up on the horizon without really taking shape. It was a dream of Roy Hofstetter's, one he kept on the backburner for a while. As it came closer to becoming reality, it almost became a nightmare. I'm talking about the dream of someday making a major Hollywood feature film about Bethany's ordeal and heroic return. It would be called *Soul Surfer*, and it was about to take us on another wild adventure.

Keeping It Real

"For I know the plans I have for you," declares
the LORD, "plans to prosper you and not to harm you,
plans to give you a hope and a future."

JEREMIAH 29:11

"Based on a true story."

We see these words in front of countless movies, but the reality is, there isn't always as much truth as there is Hollywood. When real-life events undergo transformation into a feature-length movie, truth has a strange tendency to become elastic. Early in the process, we came perilously close to being just another illustration of truth being discarded in favor of entertainment. As a family, we stood our ground, though it wasn't easy.

Making the movie *Soul Surfer* was a seven-year journey for our family. Many a movie gets shelved because no one can find the right combination of ingredients—producers, directors, actors, studios, distributors and all the rest. Roy Hofstetter, Bethany's manager, should get special credit for his persistent effort and hard work to put Bethany's story on the silver screen. He was the person who was really excited and dedicated about the whole idea of making a movie from the very beginning. The rest of us were too busy chasing waves and packing for surf competition trips. Dealing with all the other demands and changes in our lives took up a huge amount of time and energy, and we had little left over for movie-making drama!

Besides, we already had a short documentary about Bethany's story, called *The Heart of a Soul Surfer*, H.O.S.S., as we call it, which was produced and directed by Noah's wife, Becky, and documented with early surfing footage that Tom and I took while the kids were young. This work of love has been a powerful outreach tool in many different languages.

Once you have a script or story, a producer buys an "option" for a movie. (No one else can make a movie for a certain time period about Bethany's story.) During the allotted time limit, the producer tries to line up investors and studio support. But so often, these options get passed around to different producers as the time limit lapses, and the film never gets made. For our story, the first option was bought and sat on. A few meager ideas were tried, but nothing came to pass, mainly because our family refused to accept the weak and poorly written script.

Fortunately, Roy put a short time limit on the option rights. The second option bought was again sat on while a new script was written and finances raised.

Christians are too often portrayed in the movies as weirdoes, nut jobs or hypocrites. We shouldn't be surprised by this, since the Bible records in 2 Peter 3:3, "In the last days scoffers will come" (*NIV*). These are mockers who deny the truth.

None of us were interested in making a movie that would only appeal to the most hardcore believer. We wanted to share the message of hope with everyone, inside or outside of the church. As for how we wanted the faith element to be portrayed, we knew there had to be a balance. We rejected script after script because we wanted to ensure that the heart of the story remained an inspiring story about a young female athlete, Bethany, who overcame great obstacles through her faith in God. (There are several well-made movies with inspirational faith backbones. A few of my all-time favorites are *A Walk to Remember, Amazing Grace, The Mission* and *Pollyanna.*)

It took a few years before Roy was able to lock down a director along with financing. With that step, the movie suddenly had traction.

That director was Sean McNamara.

Now *Soul Surfer* was going forward, and it seemed to us that God's hand was taking care of every detail from start to finish. We believe that God assigned Sean to "direct" Bethany's life on film. Sean had a résumé with several films and lots of television work—one of which was a series about surfers shot in Hawaii called *Beyond the Break.*

When it came to the integrity of the script, Sean McNamara worked hard to sort out the good from the bad. He was clearly irritated that so many scriptwriters had set off in their own direction without regard to the real story. At six-foot-three, and with a certain presence about him, Sean sure can be intimidating to unruly screenwriters; but don't tell anyone that we think he's really a big teddy bear.

Sean took on the project because, as he said, "I wanted to make a movie that mattered." What none of us knew at the time was that making *Soul Surfer* was going to be the most challenging project in Sean's career. The job of finding someone to invest in the movie fell largely on his shoulders. He traveled all over the world, including to Dubai, Beijing and Shanghai, looking for people to back the film; but he came back empty-handed.

At the same time, there was a tug-of-war happening about the script. Sean was striving to be faithful to Bethany's story while also working with the people at Sony pictures, who warned him that he was walking a fine line by trying to please both the

Christian audience and the secular audience at the same time.

Unknown to us, Sean sometimes got to the point where he thought he should just give up. "It was a battle," he confided to us after the film had wrapped. "I felt like this project was under attack by forces that didn't want it to get out." I don't believe those were just natural or human forces. At the end of the film, he summed up the experience as one that had "tested my faith."

We were excited to have a director who was sensitive to a Christian theme, and Sean wanted to truly portray our family, not just use our characters as cardboard cutouts around the action scenes of surfing and shark attacks.

Bethany's simple yet profound faith was that faith he wanted to work into the film. Sean wanted to portray our faith in the movie as "pizza for everyone, not spinach for a few." In other words, faith is not some atypical and strange thing only for the few, but something that everyone ought to enjoy.

For all of the opposition and struggle of the early years, Sean gained some potent help from some of the key actors who were signing on. Their own vibrant faith in Christ became a bold statement for the Christian theme to remain undiluted. Through them, we gained ground in our position that our faith was an integral part of the story—without it, Bethany's amazing and dramatic comeback was meaningless.

Our insistence on the clarity and integrity of the faith element probably rubbed some people the wrong way. But as a family, we were holding on to the mission we had agreed upon many years ago: *to use our lives to glorify Christ.*

Oscar-winning actress Helen Hunt, and young actors like Ross Thomas, Lorraine Nicholson, Chris Brochu and, again, our surfer friend Sonya Balmores were signing up to be a part of the *Soul Surfer* movie—and we still didn't have a script with which we were satisfied. Finally, with the shooting scheduled only a couple of weeks away, we got the most current take on the script. While it took a few liberties, it was *finally* something we could live with—and, better yet, stand behind.

Still, at the back of our minds, we knew that even with a solid script there were a lot of hands the movie had to go through before it was shown to audiences. We could have worried about the editors, producers and studio executives, but we trusted God and we trusted who He had sent to us. We knew that Sean McNamara had the vision to keep the Christian message intact.

As I mentioned in chapter 1, once filming started, our family moved to Oahu and watched the whole thing unfold. There were a few little road bumps—some dialogue deemed "too Christian." To our surprise and joy, it was the actors and actresses who insisted on keeping the integrity of the part. And not just professed Christians like Dennis Quaid, Carrie Underwood or AnnaSophia Robb. There were many more who had the courage to speak up and keep things from getting watered down.

By the time we got to the wrap party, everyone was exhausted yet exhilarated. It felt like we had all scaled a mountain. But now we had to ride some real waves!

When the first rushes (also called dailies) of the surf scenes came in, our son Noah was not satisfied—neither were any of us, especially Bethany. The surfing scenes looked great to everyone who didn't surf. We are a family who watches surf DVDs every day, and we saw right off that we needed to showcase Bethany's surfing for an impactful ending.

Noah and Becky came up with a plan to film Bethany in Tahiti. His skeleton crew grew when everyone wanted to help out in Tahiti! He had a budget plan that tripled by the time the production team finished, but it was worth every penny spent.

It is fairly common for major film studios to have test market showings of different versions of the same movie. The test audiences fill out questionnaires so studio executives can compare audience reactions to each version. In the case of *Soul Surfer,* there was a director's cut and a studio cut. In one, the faith side of the story was stronger; in the other, the faith message was softened. For example, in one version, Dennis Quaid, playing Tom, reads to Bethany from a book clearly marked "Holy Bible." In another version, this scene might be absent altogether.

Depending on audience reaction, or perhaps studio whim, the final version of the film might be one or the other, or just have the words "Holy Bible" magically erased from the black book Dennis is holding, though he is obviously reading from the Bible. It's hard to have control over the final editing stage of the process.

Does that sound like nitpicking? Maybe. But they were making a movie about us—about real, living people—not about semilegendary figures from the past. Hollywood doesn't have the right to rewrite someone's life, unless he or she has signed that right over to them.

At least we had this first cut. Finally, our family was going to get to see the film.

The scene was Culver City, California. We were all gathered in a small theater on the lot of Sony Pictures Studios. The lights dimmed, and there on the screen was something I would have never imagined when I first stood on warm sand with a surf-board under my arm, or first noticed a handsome, goofy-foot surfer named Tom Hamilton, or first held our baby girl in my arms. There was our life being played out on a giant screen, complete with dramatic music and world-famous actors.

Have I mentioned the word "surreal" recently?

Sitting in the velvety darkness as the final credits rolled, for a moment I could see with intense clarity the hand of God working through it all. For all our fuss and fears, our tensions and tears, God had guided the making of our movie, working through believers and unbelievers alike. His hand had been on us even in our darkest hours. His hand was with Bethany, protecting her, inspiring her and blessing her with the very thing she prayed for just before the attack. Her story—her life—has proclaimed God, reaching farther than the tragedy of losing an arm, farther than if she'd never lost it.

God's hand was on Tom and me even when we were far from Him. His hand was on our unreliable van, leading us to a friend named Mark Nakatsukasa and his incredible roommates Creature and Michel, who ended up leading us to Christ. His hand guided Sarah Hill to jump feet first into youth ministry and make an impact with a bunch of rambunctious surf girls who would end up preaching the love of God across the world. God had also prompted Sarah to recall what He had written thousands of years ago—words that became our buoy of hope when the waves threatened to drown us.

Before the attack, I had so many plans for my future and dreams of how my daughter's amazing talents could affect the surfing community. But my hopes and dreams were too small for God. He always has much grander plans. Now, I was sitting in a movie theater knowing that our story, which puts God firmly in the center, would go out and reach people who maybe have never even seen an ocean. My plans were way too small. It took a tragedy to shatter them and recast them into God's plans.

Bethany's story of faith will be seen in faraway places where she may never get to visit herself. It will be bootlegged and sold for a dollar in Bali; it will be downloaded on computers and mobile devices. It will end up on Netflix and on-demand channels. Someday it might even end up on network television, with commercials for sports drinks or hair-care products interrupting the movie in weird places. It will go to people and places that would never have heard of Bethany if she had *merely* become the world champion of women's surfing.

When our plans unravel, when the fear and the tears of tragedy collapse our safe and petty world, we can only turn to God, who works all things for good to those who love Him (see Rom. 8:28). The frayed fabric of our pain becomes a work of beauty in His hands.

That day in Culver City, when the lights came on in the little theater, I saw one corner of God's tapestry, one tiny corner. It was enough.

As everyone stood and clapped, Tom and I remained seated, with tears rolling down our faces. God had used Tom and me, a couple of laid-back soul surfers with a mottled past, to raise a soul surfer for Jesus—actually, to raise a family of ocean-minded believers. Our boys have proven themselves to be men of God on their own journeys of faith. Though they may never face the same attention their little sister has, they have each honored God and their parents in their own special ways.

We are just the Hamilton family, undeserving and unworthy recipients of God's love, mercy and grace.

I am sure that the prophet Jeremiah never foresaw surfers like us when he recorded God's assuring words of care and comfort that have been our fortress of security through everything.

I like to think that our Lord was thinking of us when these words were burned into the prophet's mind: " 'For I know the plans I have for you,' declares the LORD, 'plans to prosper you and not to harm you, plans to give you hope and a future' " (Jer. 29:11, *NIV*).

Epilogue

Surfing His Waves

*They overcame him by the blood of the Lamb and by
the word of their testimony; they did not
love their lives so much as to shrink from death.*

REVELATION 12:11, *NIV*

The never-ending search for high-quality waves consumes a large amount of time and energy for avid surfers. A surfer trains to stay in shape so that one day, when that perfect swell hits, he or she will be ready to ride!

Waves generated by faraway storms can come in clean and easy to ride. A surfer can catch plenty of these and paddle back out to the lineup for more. More powerful storms can bring in bigger and better surf that becomes one of the most memorable experiences of a lifetime.

When I was in my prime of surfing, I would go out for six hours a day and not get tired. I was in shape and had strong arms from paddling into waves every day. I could make critical late takeoffs on big waves because of years of experience. But wipeouts could occur unexpectedly. One moment I was enjoying a great wave, then suddenly I was being held underwater and tossed and tumbled about, scrambling for a breath of air.

Life can be like that. One moment you are at the top of your game and the next second you are fighting for your life.

Like storms and wipeouts, adversity comes in big waves and small. Learning to take each wave at a time will exercise your inner being to strengthen and develop your resolve to survive—both spiritually and physically.

Recently, our life experiences culminated in the making of a truly amazing movie *Soul Surfer*. We went to the L.A. premiere and the party of a lifetime! We pulled up in limousines and entered through security as we viewed the words "Soul Surfer" written with lights on ponds, surfboards and other decor. Excellent food bars were spread out under the night sky, with waiters taking care of the guests' every need. A big inside room was blasting techno dance music, with a packed floor of people. Bethany and her friends danced until 2:00 A.M. After 30 years of working banquets, Tom and I have seen many elaborate parties, but this one was the best. We had VIP treatment to the max, and the only regret was not being able to invite every friend we've ever had.

We can, though, invite every person possible to an even better banquet. Jesus invites all people—great and small, rich and poor—to His upcoming Great Banquet in heaven, in His heavenly mansion where He has prepared a place for those who believe in Him. We who have trusted Him as Lord and Savior will all dine together at the greatest love feast ever—the wedding feast of the Lamb, when Jesus marries His Bride, His believers. This will be the greatest celebration ever!

This scene is described in Isaiah 25:6-9: "On this mountain the LORD Almighty will prepare a feast of rich food for all peoples, a banquet of aged wine—the best of meats and the finest of wines. On this mountain he will destroy the shroud that enfolds all peoples, the sheet that covers all nations; he will swallow up death forever. The Sovereign LORD will wipe away the tears from all faces; he will remove the disgrace of his people from all the earth. The LORD has spoken."

In the meantime, until that great day in heaven, the waves of possibility are lining up on the horizon for all of us. God is moving in our world and in our lives. We need to be ready for whatever life brings. God will send opportunities our way. And when we see them forming into waves of His purpose, we need to paddle into them and take off and ride!

There is a saying in Hawaii: "Never turn your back on the ocean." When waiting for a wave, surfers never sit staring at the beach; their eyes are on the horizon, watching for the imperceptible shift in the water that signals an incoming set. The same is true in our relationship with God. As we peer into the future, our hope is in spending eternity with Him.

EVER FELT LIKE YOU'RE IN OVER YOUR HEAD?

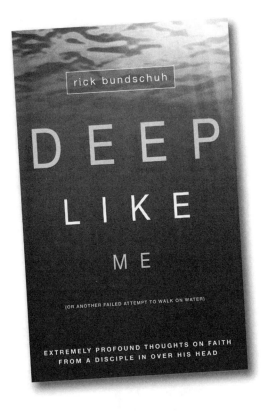

Deep Like Me
Rick Bundschuh
ISBN 978.08307.46880
ISBN 08307.46889

When people dive into the deep end of a life with Jesus, they realize before long that following in the footsteps of the Man Who Walked on Water is much more complex and challenging than just reading the Bible and minding their *P*s and *Q*s. It is a deep-sea adventure filled with wonder and difficulty, with learning and unlearning. Many soon feel like they're in over their heads (so to speak). In *Deep Like Me*, pastor Rick Bundschuh shares what he has discovered about the immersive life of faith in Jesus and invites you to wrestle, grieve, re-evaluate, redirect, focus, contemplate, be still and get real about living the deep life of a disciple. Whether you feel like you're swimming your way to a gold medal or barely keeping your head above the waves, Rick's stories of spiritual exploration are a call to leave the shallows and head for deeper water—awash in the Spirit and buoyed by grace.